EXPAND YOUR BORDERS

DISCOVER TEN CULTURAL CLUSTERS

DAVID LIVERMORE, PHD

Cultural Intelligence Center, LLC
East Lansing, Michigan

1

CQ INSIGHTS SERIES

When cultural intelligence (CQ) is increased, diverse perspectives create better solutions. The CQ Insights Series examines the specific knowledge, skills, and behaviors involved in developing cultural intelligence (CQ). The series includes resources devoted to the four capabilities of cultural intelligence (CQ Drive, CQ Knowledge, CQ Strategy, CQ Action) and other specific applications for improving and applying CQ. This is the first book in the CQ Insights Series and it's focused on improving CQ Knowledge.

© 2013 by David Livermore

Published by Cultural Intelligence Center, LLC
5337 Panda Bear Circle
East Lansing, Michigan 48823

Library of Congress, Cataloging-in-Publication Data
Livermore, David, A., 1967-
Expand your borders: discover ten cultural clusters / David Livermore
p. cm.
IISBN-13: 978-0-9897817-0-1
1. Cultural intelligence. 2. Leadership—Cross-cultural studies. 3. Cross-cultural orientation. 4. Intercultural communication. 5. Diversity in the workplace. 6. National characteristics. I. Title.
Library of Congress Control Number: 2013949361

ABOUT THE CULTURAL INTELLIGENCE CENTER
We help individuals, corporations, and organizations reach their global potential by helping them assess and develop their cultural intelligence (CQ). Visit www.culturalQ.com for more information.

Cover and Inside Design: Micah Kandros Design
Photos unless otherwise noted: Emily Livermore

CONTENTS

INTRODUCTION

My colleagues and I have spent the last several years asking the question, "What's the difference between those who are culturally intelligent and those who aren't?" Cultural intelligence, or CQ, is defined as the capability to be effective across different cultural contexts—including national, ethnic, generational, organizational, and other contexts.[1] (See Appendix A for a quick overview of cultural intelligence).

One of our key findings is that the culturally intelligent have a good grasp of overarching patterns that exist across various cultures around the world. It's not that the culturally intelligent are walking encyclopedias who can spout off random facts about any culture on the planet. That's impossible. But they have a macro understanding of cultural similarities and differences, something we identify as CQ Knowledge—one of the four capabilities of cultural intelligence. CQ Knowledge is the degree to which you understand how culture influences how people think and behave; it's also your level of familiarity with how cultures are similar and different. While this kind of understanding alone doesn't make you culturally intelligent, it is a vital part of becoming more effective across different cultural contexts.

Ten Cultural Clusters

One way to improve your CQ Knowledge is to learn the key characteristics of ten global cultural clusters, which are large cultural groupings that share some core patterns of thinking and behavior. The countries and groupings of people within each cluster typically share a common history, and they often share similar geography, language, religion, or cultural values.

Grouping people in these cultural clusters is an idea that emerged from the work of Simcha Ronen and Oded Shenkar[2], who were interested in discovering if you could map the most significant cultural groupings found across the contemporary world. Later, a group of academics drew on Ronen & Shenkar's work to conduct the GLOBE leadership project, the largest study done to date looking at leadership across cultures.[3]

These ten clusters are by no means an exact or exhaustive grouping of the thousands of cultures that exist across the world, but they provide a helpful starting point for those of us who travel widely—but not necessarily deeply—into various multicultural contexts. In the next several pages, I'm going to take you on a whirlwind tour through each of these ten clusters and give you a few snapshots of each one. We're only going to stop briefly at each place. But this kind of quick overview can help enrich your global perspective and cultural intelligence.

As we look at these ten clusters, remember that the countries listed in each are just a sampling of the ones other researchers have included in these groupings. In addition, I've assigned an icon to each cluster that we'll use to loosely describe key characteristics of many people living in that cluster.

Caution!

How does a cultural cluster evolve? It's usually the result of a combination of factors, including geography, language, religion, and history. Each cluster is a loose, but connected group that shares some general similarities. Within each of the ten clusters, plenty of differences exist. I'll point out some of the outliers and differences as we travel through these clusters. Remember, these aren't perfect classifications, but I've used the groupings created by other researchers who have spent extensive time identifying and examining these ten clusters (e.g. Ronen and Shenkar, GLOBE study, etc.).

Don't get too caught up in whether a country fits perfectly within the cluster where it's categorized. Instead, look for the broad, overarching patterns within each cluster that will give you a reference point for comparing one cultural perspective with another. You'll often meet people in these ten clusters who are a combination of multiple backgrounds. In Canada, for example, an individual may have origins in the Anglo, Sub-Saharan African and Southern Asian clusters. Or in Turkey, someone might easily share aspects of the Arab, Southern Asian, and European clusters. The ten clusters are simply a place to begin comparing one predominant worldview with another. As you develop a deeper understanding of the clusters' similarities and differences, you'll find yourself more adept at handling all kinds of intercultural situations.

As we look at each cluster, I'll offer you some practical tips for interacting effectively with its people. All of the usual cautions about not stereotyping apply here. It's dangerous to assume that all Norwegians like fish or that all Koreans prefer hierarchical leaders, but it's even more dangerous to assume that you can categorize more than seven billion people into ten general clusters. And it's never appropriate to describe an entire cultural group with negative, judgmental descriptions, such as "___ people are all lazy and corrupt."

So why even talk about clusters, and overall patterns and norms for people from various cultures? Because there's value in something that cross-cultural psychologists Joyce Osland and Allan Bird describe as "sophisticated stereotypes"—broad comparative differences based on empirical intercultural research. For example, research demonstrates that the majority of people in India prefer a more directive style to leadership, while the majority of people in Sweden don't. But you'll meet Indians working in Silicon Valley (and Delhi!) who are an anomaly to those norms. The same is true for the Swedes you meet.

Sophisticated stereotypes, such as those that stem from understanding the ten cultural clusters, are most helpful when they are:

- Used to compare various cultures rather than to understand the behavior of a singular culture

- Consciously held

- Descriptive not evaluative

- Used as a best first-guess prior to having direct information about specific people

- Modified based upon further observations and experience[4]

Sophisticated stereotypes based on the ten cultural clusters are just one part of building your CQ Knowledge. It's also helpful to learn about cultural differences that exist within generations, organizations, a country's various regions, and more. This book, however, is focused on building your CQ Knowledge by understanding the general characteristics of these ten global cultural clusters.

What To Expect
For each cluster, we're going to look at:

- An icon or cultural artifact that symbolizes the cluster in some small way

- Examples of countries included in the cluster

- An overview of the history and background of the cluster

- The cultural value dimensions that are most relevant to understanding the cluster

- Key differences within the cluster

- A few do's and taboos to consider when interacting with individuals from the cluster

In the past, I've typically shied away from providing general information about cultures, and talking about things like "do's and taboos" for different cultures. I always thought it was overly simplistic to talk about how to exchange business cards or use chopsticks. But the truth is, we don't experience cultures as theoretical constructs. We experience them through real-life interactions, where we often feel uncomfortable or wonder if we've inadvertently offended someone. If looked at with a culturally intelligent approach, understanding the general characteristics of these clusters can trigger deeper reflection and learning. And it can be a significant tool that will help you adapt to various cultures wherever you go.

The icons that I've chosen for each cluster are designed to provide a starting point for remembering a predominant characteristic of each general culture. It's not necessarily the most important characteristic of the cluster. And the icons stem from different categories—some are businesses, others are customs, and others are more conceptual. These are symbols that I've found useful while working with groups to provide a cursory introduction to the cluster. Don't over-analyze the icons. They're meant to trigger reflection and discussion as you think further about the cluster.

Since we can't possibly master the values and norms of every distinct culture in the world, and because there's diversity within all cultures, these ten cultural clusters provide a general foundation for developing your CQ Knowledge. Getting to know these ten clusters can give you a macro perspective of some of the most important cultural groupings spread across the world. Just be sure to hold them loosely and realize there will be all kinds of exceptions to the overall norms.

It's time to begin. Sit down, buckle up, and let's go around the world together.

Used with the permission of Inter IKEA Systems B.V.

1. NORDIC

EXAMPLES: Denmark, Finland, Iceland, Norway,
Sweden, etc.

ICON: IKEA

IKEA symbolizes many of the values and characteristics of the Nordic cluster. The furniture sold follows a Scandinavian approach to design— simple, minimalist, and functional. It has a contemporary, hip look with clean lines, but it's not too hip and trendy. And when you go to the store, you pick up your furniture yourself, then assemble it on your own. This is the Nordic way—minimalist, functional, and not over the top.

Our first stop is in the northernmost cultural cluster in the world. If you want to blend in while traveling in Scandinavia, you should dress neatly and sharp—but don't dress with too much bling.[1] There's a Nordic art to looking clean and neat without looking pretentious, or overly fashionable or stylish. In fact, some Scandinavians go to great lengths to ensure there isn't too much bling in their style.

Thomas Sandell, one of the most prominent Scandinavian fashion designers, says, "You can actually spend a lot of money trying to look poor here." In fact, Sandell removed the shiny bracelet from his own Rolex watch and replaced it with a simple leather band.

Can you think of anything more alien to many cultures than this idea that you aren't something special? In the U.S., parents tell their kids from the youngest age, "You're special and you can be whatever you want." A similar doting over kids exists in many European, Arab, and Asian cultures around the world. Many cultures paste bumper stickers on cars proudly declaring the success of honor roll kids. But in Nordic cultures, it's about finding ways to pursue your individual interests while making sure that everyone else has the opportunity to do that as well. Why? What's behind the Norseman who disguises the Rolex he can easily afford?

Overview

Nordic means "north," and the Nordic cluster is the ancient land and people of the Norsemen, or Vikings, as they're often called in medieval literature and history. However, the popularized caricatures of Vikings as violent brutes and savages are grossly clichéd. The name Viking actually means "men of the 'Vik,'" which is a huge area encompassing Norway and Sweden.

Wildly successful as traders, warriors, and explorers, the Vikings were skilled sailors who specialized in building robust, fast ships. During the Viking Age, physical strength, speed, resilience, and endurance were considered the most important qualities for men. Physical competition between men included wrestling, archery, javelin throwing, swimming, and skiing. They were a very active people. And while most of the Viking influence is difficult to spot in Scandinavia today, the love for the outdoors, the enjoyment of sports, and an emphasis on making the most of life by the sea all stem from the cluster's Viking roots.

Jante Law is one of the most important ideas to understand about the Nordic cluster. This is an idea made popular by Danish author Aksel Sandemose back in the 1930s. Sandemose wrote a novel called *A Fugitive Crosses His Tracks* and, for the purposes of his novel, he created a small Danish town called Jante, a place where nobody is anonymous. The town of Jante was governed by ten rules, or Jante Law.

The overarching rule of Jante Law is this: "Don't think you're anything special." It's hard to overstate how strongly this idea weaves through the Nordic cultures. Modesty, equality, humility, and skepticism are all expressions of Jante Law. Everyone is on equal footing and each citizen—and society as a whole—should do whatever it can to protect that right.

Jante Law can be seen in the design world of Nordic culture. This is true whether we're talking about furniture, architecture, or fashion. Things look hip and cool, but there's an underlying theme of minimalism and functionalism. Just think of some of the most noteworthy Swedish brands: Volvo cars, IKEA furniture, and H&M clothes. In all these brands, you see functional, straight lines. There's good quality, but it's not over the top. It's crisp and clean, but it blends in with the landscape. Bang & Olufsen, the Danish manufacturer of audio-video equipment, prides itself on taking minimalism to an extreme. The functionalism and minimalism seen in Nordic design is a reflection of Jante Law: Don't think you're something special!

Cultural Value Dimensions

People living in Nordic countries have been largely shaped by an environment that forces them to survive cold, harsh conditions. Summers are short and winters have limited periods of sunshine, and many months of snow and cold. This comes through in the dominant norms, or "cultural value dimensions," of this cluster.

I'll use the following seven cultural values to describe and compare the ten clusters as we move around the world. If you aren't familiar with these terms, I've provided a bit of background on them in Appendix B, as well as a chart that shows you how each of the ten clusters compares along these seven cultural values.

Cultural Value Definitions   **Nordic**

INDIVIDUALISM-COLLECTIVISM   Individualist
Individualism: Individual goals and rights are more
important than personal relationships.

Collectivism: Personal relationships and benefiting the
group are more important than individual goals.

POWER DISTANCE   Low
Low Power Distance: Status differences are of little   Power
importance; empowered decision-making is expected   Distance
across all levels.

High Power Distance: Status differences should shape
social interactions; those with authority should make
decisions.

UNCERTAINTY AVOIDANCE

Low Uncertainty Avoidance: Focus on flexibility and adaptability; tolerant of unstructured and unpredictable situations.

High Uncertainty Avoidance: Focus on planning and reliability; uncomfortable with unstructured or unpredictable situations.

Low Uncertainty Avoidance

COOPERATIVE-COMPETITITVE

Cooperative: Emphasis on cooperation and nurturing behavior; high value placed on relationships and family.

Competitive: Emphasis on assertive behavior and competition; high value placed on work, task accomplishment, and achievement.

Cooperative

TIME ORIENTATION

Short-Term: Values immediate outcomes more than long-term benefits (success now).

Long-Term: Values long-term planning; willing to sacrifice short-term outcomes for long-term benefits (success later).

Short-Term Time

CONTEXT

Low Context: Values direct communication; emphasis on explicit words.

High Context: Values indirect communication; emphasis on harmonic relationships and implicit understanding.

Low Context

BEING-DOING

Being: Social commitments and task completion are equally important; diffuse boundaries between personal and work activities.

Doing: Task completion takes precedence over social commitments; clear separation of personal and work activities.

Being

See Appendix B for comparison with other clusters.

While understanding all of these cultural value dimensions is important, the following values are particularly significant for driving culturally intelligent interaction with people from the countries in the Nordic cluster.

Individualist

There's an independent streak across the Nordic cluster. Norway remains outside the European Union, and Denmark and Sweden have stayed clear of the Euro. The people across this cluster are moderately Individualist, meaning there's a commitment to allow each person to do as they wish, with some attention to collective interest.

This moderate level of individualism renders the Nordic cluster different from the other Individualist clusters (e.g. Anglo or Germanic). The emphasis on Jante Law discourages a person from standing out independently, which sounds more Collectivist than Individualist. And institutionally-speaking, the Nordic cluster could be considered more Collectivist because there's greater attention placed upon the needs of the whole than what you usually find in Individualist cultures. But the priority of not thinking you're something special is to ensure that everyone gets a chance to pursue his or her individual interests. So the greatest concern is promoting autonomy and individual choice. And society is built around protecting the rights of the individual.

Power Distance

As in most Individualist cultures, the Nordic countries are very Low Power Distance. They resist hierarchy and they avoid creating distinctions between people according to status. Jante Law is built upon an egalitarian ethos. Leaders downplay directive, authoritative styles and there's great distaste for inequality. Respect and influence are gained through character and performance, not title and status.

Cooperative and Being

Nothing repels Nordic voters like aggressive politicians. Even in its most cantankerous form, Nordic politics are like a gentle disagreement among friends. The Nordic people prefer to accomplish goals through collaboration and by treating one another respectfully. This ties closely with the Nordic preference for Being over Doing. Being is the cultural dimension that most strongly sets apart the Nordic culture from other European cultures. There's a strong belief in the importance of working to live rather than living to work.

Nordic culture, while certainly pursuing many business interests, is committed first and foremost to enhancing people's quality of life. Most Nordic businesses are closed for the month of July. In fact, 20 percent of police stations close down during the summer months because so few people remain in the cities. In Sweden, all employees (including grad students) get five weeks of paid vacation. And if they want, Swedish employees have to be allowed to take three of those weeks consecutively. The Nordic cultures also have the most generous family-leave policies of any cluster in the world, some providing up to three years leave between the father and mother of a newly born child.

The Nordic emphasis on working less is not just because these countries want to be generous to their workers. They actually believe they'll build a better society when people have a well-rounded life. Those in Doing cultures often look at someone who puts in twelve-hour workdays as someone who is really committed and hard working. Someone from a Nordic culture would typically look at an individual like that as being sadly incompetent, perhaps thinking, *Too bad they don't have the skill set to get their job done in six or seven hours*. They're very committed to working smarter, not harder. And the driving objective is to do so in order to enjoy life. You work to live.

Key Differences

During our stop in the Nordic cluster, it's important to note some of the differences that exist within the Nordic countries. In fact, there's a significant amount of competition among the nations in this cluster. Norwegians tell jokes about the Swedes and vise versa. When you travel in this part of the world, you'll find that the people will appreciate your understanding that they aren't all the same—and it's worth asking them about some of the differences.

The functionalism described earlier is seen most among the Finns. They're the kings of the practical, functional style. They prefer to develop and use the most stripped-down version of what's needed. Get rid of unnecessary frills. Swedes, not quite as functionally driven as the Finns, have more concern about aesthetic value, though their commitment to Jante Law certainly remains strong.

On the whole, Swedes are more comfortable with silence during communication, as compared to Norwegians who typically aren't. But both cultures are very direct in their communication. And Danes are typically the most direct of all the Nordic cultures.[2]

Do's and Taboos

- If you're traveling to the Nordic region on business, punctuality for meetings is extremely important. Scandinavians are terribly worried about wasting other people's time. They have a limited amount of time to do their job, so efficiency is everything for the Nordic people.

- If you want to blend in, dress neatly and limit the bling. Work toward being understated in your dress and overall demeanor.

- Be precise and clear with your communication, and don't exaggerate.

- Even though work/life balance is very important, Nordic people will likely focus conversation on your job first; because they can be a little socially shy, they will find it easier to speak about your job before discussing personal matters.

- There tends to be a more relaxed attitude toward nudity throughout the Nordic world than in many other places. Don't be surprised to see nude people at the beach. Saunas, a favorite Nordic tradition, are generally visited in the nude.

- Nordic couples are usually more independent than what is typical in many other cultures. A husband and wife are often expected to have at least some separate friendships. In Scandinavia, it's perfectly fine for a married person to go out to a café or for drinks with someone they aren't married to. So beware of assuming too much about what's going on if you observe this happening.

- Nordic cultures tend to be very irreligious and sometimes even anti-religious. It's not that Nordic people as a whole see religion as a bad thing. It's just that religion is something that most people don't take part in or really understand as having much relevance to real life.

- Remember that not everyone in this cluster will fit these descriptions! These general patterns are just a starting point. Be sure to look for exceptions when you interact with people from the Nordic cluster.

Photo Credit: Alexandra Vlettl

2. ANGLO

EXAMPLES: Australia, Canada, Ireland, New Zealand, U.K., U.S., etc.

ICON: Deodorant

Hygiene and deodorant are important to many people around the world. But nowhere are personal space and hygiene as highly valued as in the Anglo Cluster, the next stop in our tour around the world.

Anglo cultures originated primarily in places where wide-open land was the norm, so people settled with a great deal of room between them and their neighbors. Anglos like their space. Being close to someone's face is reserved for intimacy with loved ones, otherwise it's perceived as an act of aggression—as in, he was really "in my face."

One time I was visiting a Ukrainian family in their home in Odessa. Like most of us, they had a variety of knick-knacks displayed throughout their apartment. Their living room shelves were filled with mementos from different countries and cultures. I was looking at a beautiful set of matryoshka dolls—the small stacking dolls that nest one inside the other—when I noticed that, sitting next to the dolls, was a stick of deodorant. I was very curious why they had this displayed in their living room.

Eventually I asked them about it and they explained that the deodorant had been left behind by another North American visitor. They thought it was so interesting that we spend money to keep ourselves from sweating, and work hard to disguise our natural odor, that they decided it would be fun to display the deodorant for others to see. It had become quite the conversation piece for them.

There are plenty of people around the world who use deodorant, including many Ukrainians. But the Anglo cultures place an unusually high priority upon personal space, hygiene, autonomy, and achievement. Why? What's behind the Anglo way of life?

Overview

Stopping to visit this cluster is a bit more challenging, because the Anglo cluster is the most geographically dispersed of the ten cultural clusters in our worldwide tour. But what unites the Anglo cluster most is a shared ethnic and linguistic history—Caucasians who speak English. The Anglo ancestors migrated several centuries ago from the Nordic and Germanic worlds into modern day Britain. In 410 A.D., Rome removed Its army from Britain, and the population that remained struggled for power. By the latter half of the 5th century A.D., the Germanic Oisc gained kingship and bequeathed the name of the Oisingas on the Kentish, British royal household. This was a key part of establishing the British royal monarchy and the Anglo cluster.

The Anglo population is relatively small on a global scale. It accounts for roughly seven percent of the world yet it represents forty percent of the world's GDP. So most of the world has been strongly influenced by the Anglo cluster in significant ways. A great deal of the Anglo imprint across the globe stems from its long history of expanding its reach by colonizing other parts of the world.[1]

John Darwin, in his book *Unfinished Empire: The Global Expansion of Britain*[2], suggests that one of the surprising things about the British Empire is that it didn't begin with any unifying vision. But that lack of unifying vision actually reflects one of the most important nuances of the empire and of the Anglo cluster. Britain was an unusually pluralistic and intellectually open society, compared to what was going on elsewhere in the 17th and 18th centuries. Their ruthless independence, combined with an obsession with expansion, gave them a matchless ability to build and self-promote wherever they went. From India to Malaysia to countries all across Africa, British emperors managed to get the indigenous people they colonized to be collaborators in their own colonization. While they came into a new country with their own institutions and philosophies, the Brits believed a successful colony had to allow the local people to retain some aspect of their individuality. They presumed that people would want to have some autonomy.

Cultural Value Dimensions

Nearly all of the Anglo nations have frontier lands in the western and central part of their countries. And most of them have oceans on both sides of their borders, further reinforcing their ruthless, independent spirit and desire for space. Again we see historical and geographical influences that shape the values found across the Anglo cluster today.

Cultural Value Definitions

Anglo

INDIVIDUALISM-COLLECTIVISM | Individualist

Individualism: Individual goals and rights are more important than personal relationships.

Collectivism: Personal relationships and benefiting the group are more important than individual goals.

POWER DISTANCE | Low Power Distance

Low Power Distance: Status differences are of little importance; empowered decision-making is expected across all levels.

High Power Distance: Status differences should shape social interactions; those with authority should make decisions.

UNCERTAINTY AVOIDANCE | Low Uncertainty Avoidance

Low Uncertainty Avoidance: Focus on flexibility and adaptability; tolerant of unstructured and unpredictable situations.

High Uncertainty Avoidance: Focus on planning and reliability; uncomfortable with unstructured or unpredictable situations.

COOPERATIVE-COMPETITITVE | Competitive

Cooperative: Emphasis on cooperation and nurturing behavior; high value placed on relationships and family.

Competitive: Emphasis on assertive behavior and competition; high value placed on work, task accomplishment, and achievement.

TIME ORIENTATION *Short-Term:* Values immediate outcomes more than long-term benefits (success now). *Long-Term:* Values long-term planning; willing to sacrifice short-term outcomes for long-term benefits (success later).	Short-Term Time
CONTEXT *Low Context:* Values direct communication; emphasis on explicit words. *High Context:* Values indirect communication; emphasis on harmonic relationships and implicit understanding.	Low Context
BEING-DOING *Being:* Social commitments and task completion are equally important; diffuse boundaries between personal and work activities. *Doing:* Task completion takes precedence over social commitments; clear separation of personal and work activities.	Doing
See Appendix B for comparison with other clusters.	

While understanding all of these cultural value dimensions is important, the following values are particularly significant for driving culturally intelligent interaction with people from the countries in the Anglo cluster.

Individualist

If I had to choose one cultural value that most strongly characterizes the Anglo cluster, it would be individualism. The Anglo cultures are largely organized around the idea of individual rights, freedom, and responsibility. Roman Law declared that all should be equal, and the Anglo cluster was built on this premise. Free speech is an extremely important value, which reflects the cluster's priority on protecting individual rights.

Furthermore, the Anglo cluster does not have, nor does it want, much emphasis on group loyalty and collective interests. The priority is most definitely upon individual goals and interests. People need to be allowed to struggle for self-reliance and to work hard to gain personal material possessions.

If the Anglo cluster is Individualist, the U.S. culture is the extreme version of individualism. In fact, it's been said that every U.S. politician wants you to believe he was born into poverty and built a log cabin all by himself.

This heavy emphasis upon individualism helps explain the customs in Anglo cultures related to personal space. Most Anglos feel threatened and violated when someone gets too close—and on the rare occasion when it's necessary, the person invading their personal space better at least smell okay!

Competitive and Doing

Another guiding principle for life in the Anglo world is "quid pro quo." Anglos believe there should always be give and take. There's a reluctance to ask people for something unless there's an ability to return the favor. There's a high priority placed on not being an imposition, but also on not having others impose on you. It's all about creating win/win relationships and partnerships. So if I ask you to do something for me, I have to think about how I will pay you, or what's in this for you.

The Competitive orientation of the Anglo cluster is closely linked to the high Doing orientation. "Actions speak louder than words" is a mantra of Anglo life. The Competitive, Doing values of the Anglo cluster are seen in the British Empire's devout loyalty to the principles of Greece's Achilles. Achilles' driving goal was to impose his will on the world. The British Empire took this philosophy to heart—far beyond what the Greeks themselves did. The British Empire was intent on dominating the world, believing it had the world's best interests at heart.

Short-Term Time Orientation

Finally, the Anglo cluster has a relatively Short-Term Time Orientation. This stems from the Individualist, competitive nature of the cluster. Quick wins are important, and there's very little patience for long-term, twenty-year ideas. These cultures are interested in performance that can achieve results now or in the very near future.

Key Differences

Baxter Black, a self-described American cowboy, is a radio commentator and journalist who likens Anglo countries to a large extended family. Britain is the mother of the family and each of the other Anglo countries are her children.[3]

Canada might be described as the child most like it's mother. There's far more interest in the British royal family in Canada than there is in the U.S. In Canada, you often see the queen's picture prominently displayed in public places, and Canadians are much more focused on the comings and goings of the royal family than most of the other Anglo children are.

The U.S. might be described as the child who ran away and became successful. He eventually came back to visit and the family took him in. The U.S. and Mother England have to work together because everyone expects it of them—but there's some tension in the relationship. And instead of pictures of the queen, Americans are more likely to display posters of Princess Di with Michael Jackson.

Baxter says Australia might be thought of as the resentful but dependent child of Mother England. Australia was a difficult adolescent and Mother

England didn't spare the rod. Baxter compares Australia to the kid who had much less interest in college, politics, or business than in life at the beach. But the Australians are loyal and steadfast to the British tradition when it comes to sports, tea parties, and eating organ meats and meat pies. And Baxter thinks the Aussies would be a lot more fun at a family reunion than the dogmatic Americans or the pompous Brits.

The relationship between the U.K. and Ireland is perhaps more like a strained relationship between cousins. And some might question whether Ireland should even be included in the Anglo cluster given the long historical differences between the two places. But it has more affinity with the Anglo cluster than any other cluster, so it makes sense to at least loosely place it here.

Like most families, there's some resemblance among the family members, but each one goes about life a bit differently. However, despite the differences and internal fighting, Anglo countries are quick to defend each other when an outsider picks on one of them.

Do's and Taboos

- Be on time. Time is money in the Anglo world and you will be judged severely based on punctuality.

- Don't ask people how much money they make. This is something that is freely talked about in some cultures, but not in the Anglo world. Money is a very individual, private thing and not something talked about with just anyone.

- Gift giving is not necessary when meeting a new business acquaintance. Just be friendly and enjoy yourself. In fact, giving a gift too soon in a business relationship might be seen as manipulative or as a bribe.

- Allow for plenty of personal space, particularly when meeting a stranger. There's limited physical contact between Anglo men, and while kissing on the cheek between men and women is sometimes done in places like the East Coast of the U.S., as a whole it's not the norm in Anglo cultures.

- Most people in Anglo cultures are very leery of imposing on anyone. If you're making a request of someone, be respectful of how they define personal boundaries, and be careful in the way you ask.

- Remember that not everyone in this cluster will fit these descriptions! Not all Anglos are the same.

3. GERMANIC

EXAMPLES: Austria, Belgium, Germany, Netherlands, German-Switzerland, etc.

ICON: Quiet Hours

There's a longstanding law in Germany that says, "A homeowner should enjoy his/her property in such a way as to not have a detrimental effect on his/her neighbors." This law, commonly referred to as "quiet hours," plays out differently in various states across Germany, but, typically, it means that everyone needs to remain quiet from 8 p.m. to 6 a.m. daily, all day Sunday, and on holidays. And in many German states, quiet hours also include 1-3 p.m. every weekday afternoon. During quiet hours in Germany, you may not mow the lawn, drop glass bottles in a recycling bin, rev your car engine, blast loud music, or run the washing machine if you live in an apartment building. This isn't one of those crazy laws that never get applied. It's widely expected that people will follow these rules, and German judges review numerous violations of quiet hours in their courts each month.

One time I was checking into a hotel in Austria, and the person at the front desk asked me what time I would like my room cleaned the next morning. I looked at her, a little confused. "I have to give you a time?"

I had several meetings the next day, but I didn't have the exact times confirmed yet, so I told the desk clerk, "Anytime in the morning is fine. If I'm working in my room, they can just work around me, or I'll step out for a few minutes." She insisted they needed an exact time so I said, "Okay, let's say 9 a.m."

The next morning, I ended up working in my room because some of my meetings had been rescheduled. Late in the day, my room still hadn't been cleaned, so I went to the front desk to ask about it. The same woman was there and she said, "That's because you weren't out of your room at 9:00." I said, "Okay. Well can someone clean it now?" She responded, "No, the cleaning staff leaves at noon. What time would you like it cleaned tomorrow?" And the cycle started all over again.

From my North American perspective, the customer is always right. But from the Germanic perspective, I was staying in their hotel and they have rules and procedures. If I want to stay there, I agree to respect the way they run their hotel, and I either abide by their rules or I suffer the consequences. To be clear, I've stayed in many hotels across the Germanic world where they clean my room much like they would in hotels located in other places, so I'm not suggesting this hotel policy was typical. But the idea that there are rules and policies to regulate life is a very Germanic characteristic. This is why I view the "quiet hours" rule in Germany as emblematic of the next cluster on our journey around the world—Germanic Europe.

Overview

The Germanic cluster has a long, rich heritage. If you don't understand and appreciate some of the values and history behind the norms and rules you encounter, you can falsely interpret German behavior as being legalistic, distant, and even untrusting.

Germanic Europe dates all the way back to Charles the Great's reign in the 8th Century. Some historians say you can find a distinctive German culture as far back as 5400 B.C. When Tacitus, the Roman writer, published Germania around 100 A.D., he described the Germanic cultural tribe as a group of people who possess a love of freedom and fighting.

It was during Charlemagne's reign that the Germanic cluster began to emerge as a united empire stretching across Western Europe. The Habsburg Dynasty, which originated in Switzerland, dominated Austria's history from the 13th century to the beginning of the 20th century. The Habsburgs were very successful in enlarging their territories, which they accomplished primarily through strategic marriages to key leaders of other areas. After the marriage, the Habsburgs would take over the region, adding it to their empire.

The historical development of The Netherlands followed a different course from that of the other Germanic nations. Conquered by a Spanish line of the Habsburgs, The Netherlands evolved with distinctive differences from Austria and Germany. But, like Germany and Austria, The Netherlands was also part of what eventually became known as the Holy Empire of the German Nation.

Germanic culture is resistant to quick change. Even while Eastern Germany was under Communist rule for forty years, the people and institutions throughout the country retained the long-standing Germanic values. While different generations and circumstances have influenced how values and customs have been expressed, the orderliness, straight-forward approach, and loyalty found in Germanic culture have characterized the people here for many centuries. Germanic Europe is a relatively tight culture that is slow to change.

The Germanic cluster is comparatively small in size, but it has a huge economic footprint in the world, and the countries in this cluster have deep economic ties with each another. Germany is only behind China and the U.S. as the world's biggest exporter. The Swiss are famous for their wildly successful banking industry, and The Netherlands, an incredibly small country, is a formidable economic power in its own right, and it has been for centuries. From the late 16th century, the Dutch Empire was a major force in the world, largely as a result of their success in shipping and trading. Even today, Rotterdam is the largest European port, and the third largest in the world—only Shanghai and Singapore are bigger.

The cluster's economic strength is primarily the result of its expertise in foreign trade, and production of high-quality, innovative products; there are relatively few natural resources within its own borders. Rigorous thinking, insistence on quality control, and tenacity all contribute to the financial fortitude that has typically characterized these cultures. The financial strength of the cluster makes Germanic people all the more confident in their way of life being a proven, effective way to live.[1]

Another key factor in understanding the Germanic cluster is recognizing the influence of its cultural leaders: Germany is historically a land of poets, novelists, musicians, and philosophers. For centuries, Germany was the cultural center of Europe, with Goethe, Beethoven, Wagner, and the Grimm Brothers serving as instantly recognizable contributors to not only German culture but to civilization as a whole.

Though Germany is now the industrial heart of Central Europe, the arts continue to permeate German life. Most primary schools and high schools require students to learn a musical instrument, and study humanities and poetry alongside their rigorous classes in math and science.

Cultural Value Dimensions

The cultural values in the Germanic cluster run strong and deep. The long history of the cluster, combined with the people's confidence in their approach to life, makes the Germanic way of life very distinctive—though you'll always meet individuals who are exceptions.

Cultural Value Definitions

Germanic

INDIVIDUALISM-COLLECTIVISM

Individualism: Individual goals and rights are more important than personal relationships.

Collectivism: Personal relationships and benefiting the group are more important than individual goals.

Individualist

POWER DISTANCE

Low Power Distance: Status differences are of little importance; empowered decision-making is expected across all levels.

High Power Distance: Status differences should shape social interactions; those with authority should make decisions.

Low
Power
Distance

UNCERTAINTY AVOIDANCE

Low Uncertainty Avoidance: Focus on flexibility and adaptability; tolerant of unstructured and unpredictable situations.

High Uncertainty Avoidance: Focus on planning and reliability; uncomfortable with unstructured or unpredictable situations.

Moderate
Uncertainty
Avoidance

COOPERATIVE-COMPETITITVE

Cooperative: Emphasis on cooperation and nurturing behavior; high value placed on relationships and family.

Competitive: Emphasis on assertive behavior and competition; high value placed on work, task accomplishment, and achievement.

Competitive

TIME ORIENTATION

Short-Term: Values immediate outcomes more than long-term benefits (success now).

Long-Term: Values long-term planning; willing to sacrifice short-term outcomes for long-term benefits (success later).

Moderate
Time

CONTEXT	Low
Low Context: Values direct communication; emphasis on explicit words.	Context
High Context: Values indirect communication; emphasis on harmonic relationships and implicit understanding.	
BEING-DOING	Doing
Being: Social commitments and task completion are equally important; diffuse boundaries between personal and work activities.	
Doing: Task completion takes precedence over social commitments; clear separation of personal and work activities.	
See Appendix B for comparison with other clusters.	

All of the cultural value dimensions have relevance for understanding the Germanic cluster, but the following are particularly significant when it comes to interacting with cultural intelligence with people from the countries in this cluster.

Individualist
While not as Individualist as the Anglo cluster, Germanic Europe is certainly more Individualist than Collectivist. The abundance of rules and regulations are meant to protect the rights of the individual. And in the workplace, companies are expected to have explicit policies for how individual employees can voice complaints and concerns. Companies must also provide flexibility for individuals to pursue community and civic interests that go beyond their work responsibilities.[2]

Power Distance
Even though rules and procedures are important, the cluster is quite Low Power Distance. The culture frowns upon making big distinctions in status between people functioning at different levels.

Think for a moment about German Chancellor Angela Merkel. Merkel and her husband live in a modest flat in Berlin. There's very little pomp and circumstance around their public appearances. And Merkel's husband, a quiet chemistry professor, often flies budget airlines to join his wife on holidays. This reflects the Low Power Distance of the Germanic culture.

Uncertainty Avoidance

Uncertainty Avoidance is the cultural dimension that most uniquely characterizes the Germanic cluster, particularly as you compare it with other Western cultures such as those found in the Nordic or Anglo clusters. Rules and policies are created to help reduce the chance that things will get out of control. Germanics tend to buy many different kinds of insurance to avoid risk at all cost. Order is highly valued. The typical German home is very neat and tidy, and the various government districts across the country have numerous rules about how homes and yards must be maintained.

The Germans are masters of security and careful planning. By having rules about things like quiet hours, they guarantee that everyone can be assured some quiet rest and peacefulness at set times everyday. This is the preferred way of life in the Germanic culture—predictable and structured.

Competitive and Doing

The Germanic cluster scores high on the Competitive index. People here are very focused on results and winning. Punctuality is king; following schedules is one more way to reduce uncertainty. There's a good reason why Germans and Swiss make clocks and watches! The contrast of German train schedules with French or Italian train schedules couldn't be more obvious. The orientation toward Doing is also very high in the cluster. There tends to be a higher commitment to tasks and to staying focused on the task at hand than to attending to one's well-being and quality of life.

Low Context

Communication is very Low Context and direct among the Germanic people. There's a German saying, "Da muss man mal Deutsch sprechen," which translates, "Sometimes one has to talk German"—meaning sometimes you need to stop beating around the bush and openly voice an opinion. You can expect most Germanic people to be clear, explicit, and blunt. The Moderate Uncertainty Avoidance combined with the direct approach to communication across these countries may also explain why social interactions tend to be more formal until you get to know someone better. There's definitely a protocol to how relationships evolve.

Key Differences

Austria, Switzerland, and Germany are neighboring countries where German is a predominant language. However, understand that Austrians dislike being called Germans! And there are significant regions within Switzerland that fit more closely with the Latin European cluster, given their strong French and Italian influences.

The biggest outlier in this cluster is The Netherlands. The Netherlands shares a border with Germany, but it's sometimes grouped with the Nordic cluster because of both its location and its strong ties to the fishing and shipping industries. And Holland is much more loose in its acceptance of different norms and values than the other Germanic countries. Also, The Netherlands is a very Cooperative culture as compared to the more Competitive orientation of the Germanic cluster as a whole. Finally, Dutch (albeit a language of German origin), not German, is the predominant language of The Netherlands.

Despite these differences, most cross-cultural experts agree that The Netherlands fits best with the Germanic cluster. Again, for the time being, we're more interested in general, over-arching patterns found around the world than a deep analysis of specific national cultures.

 Do's and Taboos

- In contrast to many cultures around the world, Germanic people thrive on a good debate, and even a hearty discussion of politics and faith. So if you're up for it, dive into a meaningful discussion about this with people you meet. And keep in mind that you're often respected more when you disagree, assuming there's substance to your point of view.

- Don't disparage academics. While there's an anti-Intellectualism that often permeates the business and professional world in many contexts, the Germanic cluster holds academic research and intellectual inquiry in high regard. They love to see a CEO have a PhD. And many Germanic universities require two doctorates before one can teach at a university.

- The laws about quiet hours probably won't affect you if you're simply a tourist. But do be conscious of your volume, particularly later in the evening.

- When you're meeting someone, expect intense eye contact and a firm hand shake with a slight nod of the head—that's a typical Germanic greeting.

- Remember that not everyone in this cluster will fit these descriptions! Look for and expect some exceptions as you meet people in the Germanic region.

4. EASTERN EUROPE

EXAMPLES: Bulgaria, Czech Republic, Estonia, Hungary, Kazakhstan, Mongolia, Poland, Russia, Serbia, etc.

ICON: Matryoshka Doll

Walk into nearly any souvenir shop in our next cluster and you'll see matryoshka dolls for sale—the small, round stacking dolls that nest inside each other. The dolls now appear in various places around the world, but they're believed to have first emerged in Russia in the late 1800s. The most traditional versions of the dolls are of a sturdy peasant mother and her similar looking children. Historians believe this represents the matriarchal family model that has existed across this region for centuries. The mother tended to her children while the father was out working the land or fighting off the latest invaders. As you open one doll after another, there's a sense of uncertainty and surprise about whether this will be the last one. In many ways, the dolls are a perfect symbol for a region that's gone through constant transitions, endless periods of "uncertainty and surprise."

It's 10:30 at night and I'm sitting in a traffic jam. I just finished dinner at a Mexican restaurant with a group of colleagues and new acquaintances. It seems like the city is in constant motion, with people everywhere. And as I look around, I'm struck by all the glitzy shopping centers and high-end hotels that have gone up since the last time I was here.

The sidewalks are full of people walking around with bags from Burberry and Gucci. Everyone is using a smart phone. Hummers and luxury cars are driving by. The bizarre thing is, when I was here a few years ago there were virtually no chain stores or restaurants. And all the hotels looked gray and grimy. Where do you think I am?

I suppose my description could define any number of places I've been around the world, but I'm in a place that has often been called "the end of the world." I'm describing my experience in Ulan Bator, Mongolia, sometimes referred to as the "Timbuktu of the East." This is the land of Genghis Khan where, until very recently, there were more horses on the streets than there were cars. But in recent years, Mongolia has experienced double-digit GDP growth, a soaring stock market, and an influx of investors from London, Dubai, and Dallas.

But as soon as you leave the capital city, the outskirts of Ulan Bator look very much like they have for several centuries. You see nomadic tent communities where people live in poverty and where there's little sign of modern-day civilization. And the city backs up against the vast Gobi Desert—one of the most extreme ecosystems in the world. Mongolia is part of the Eastern European cluster, a vast expanse of widely diverse countries and people that spreads across Europe and parts of Asia.[1] Perhaps the only unifying characteristic of this cluster is that it includes a collection of societies that have been in continual transition for several centuries. This is a place where families have had a long history of needing to pick up and move at a moment's notice in order to survive the threats of Mother Nature or the newest group of colonizers.

Overview

Eastern Europe, our next stop, is a much more diverse cluster than the ones we've visited so far. In fact, my friends and colleagues from Russia, Poland, and Mongolia are baffled that this vast region of varied cultures can even be talked about as one unified cluster. And I see their point: It's the cluster where I've had the greatest challenge understanding why early researchers grouped these vastly different cultures into one cluster. But to be consistent with the framework and research that is the basis of the ten clusters, I'll highlight a couple of the historical characteristics shared across this cluster and suggest some considerations for interacting with people from this region.

The Eastern European cultures were most strongly influenced by the Byzantine Empire. The Roman Empire primarily moved west of the Mediterranean Sea, and the Byzantine Empire primarily moved east. As with everything else in this region, the depth of influence from the Byzantine Empire varies widely across the cluster. For example, you clearly see the influence of the eastward migration of the Byzantines through the strong presence of the Orthodox Church throughout many of the nations in the Eastern European cluster. This is nowhere more evident than in Russia. The Russian Orthodox Church is the largest of the Eastern Orthodox Churches in the world. Yet in Poland and Lithuania, the Catholic Church has a much larger presence, indicating that these countries were more strongly influenced by the Roman Empire.

Another thing for us to consider while we stop in the Eastern European cluster is the impact of its long, relentless history of colonization. Sometimes the colonizing forces came from outside regions, while other times was led by various groups within the cluster. Whether we look at the Empires of Ottoman and Prussia, or the Mongols and Tatars, or the Soviets, most of the nations in this cluster faced significant periods of domination—or, they themselves were attempting to dominate their neighbors. While this cycle is apparent in most cultures around the world, the frequency with which this has occurred within this cluster is above and beyond what happened elsewhere. Nearly all of the countries in the cluster were once part of larger, more powerful empires, and they didn't become independent until after WWI. So amidst the vast diversity that exists in Hungary, Russia, and Mongolia, there's an underlying shared experience that comes from their histories with colonization. As a result, even to this day, the ability for communities and families to quickly mobilize and adapt in a short amount of time is perhaps the most significant characteristic of the Eastern European cluster, as seen in groups as diverse as modern-day Russians, Kazaks, and Turks.

Many of the countries in this region have experienced significant geopolitical changes numerous times within our lifetime. Consequently, many of the people living in this cluster have more loyalty to their ethnic identity than to the arbitrary geopolitical nations they've ended up calling home.

When they weren't trying to throw off the shackles of colonization, Eastern Europeans were trying to escape Mother Nature. Much of the region is characterized by harsh terrain and weather. The temperatures in Mongolia, for example, range from −57°F in the winter to 96°F in the summer. The biggest weather extremes are in Mongolia and Siberia, but harsh summers and winters are characteristic of many of the countries included in this cluster. For centuries, the societies living across this region were forced to navigate these extreme geographical and weather conditions. In some cases, their survival required a nomadic lifestyle, constantly moving from one place to the next, trying to escape the harshest elements of winter and summer.

Over the last fifteen years, extreme development has wrought so much change in this region that it's become difficult to find much that's consistent across the cluster. But in most of the cultures included in Eastern Europe, you continue to find a survivalist mentality. As a result, people can quickly mobilize in light of whatever difficult circumstances they face.

While some people in this cluster have nomadic roots, others come from descendants who set up homesteads and trading posts in towns and cities across the region. But when nomads and townspeople had to co-exist, there was a great deal of tension. The nomads envied the townspeople for the conveniences of modern life and stability; at times, the nomads decided the only way to survive was to invade and plunder the towns.

That same tense situation is playing out today in Mongolia. The reason Ulan Bator is now filled with luxury cars, high-fashion retailers, and an influx of foreign investors is because of the discovery of an ocean of coal that lies beneath the sandy earth in Mongolia. And so the cycle continues. One must be tough with outsiders, but there's an abundance of hospitality toward one's own kin and clan. While it takes a long time to trust other clans, if and when you do, you welcome them in as one of your own.

Cultural Value Dimensions

The weather, geography, and historical conquests experienced by the Eastern European people deeply shaped them. Visitors are often confused by people in these countries who can appear, on one hand, to be cool and aloof, yet who can also exude the warm hospitality symbolized by that plump mother matryoshka doll.

Cultural Value Definitions	Eastern Europe
INDIVIDUALISM-COLLECTIVISM *Individualism:* Individual goals and rights are more important than personal relationships. *Collectivism:* Personal relationships and benefiting the group are more important than individual goals.	Moderate Collectivist
POWER DISTANCE *Low Power Distance:* Status differences are of little importance; empowered decision-making is expected across all levels. *High Power Distance:* Status differences should shape social interactions; those with authority should make decisions.	Moderate* Power Distance

UNCERTAINTY AVOIDANCE

Low Uncertainty Avoidance: Focus on flexibility and adaptability; tolerant of unstructured and unpredictable situations.

High Uncertainty Avoidance: Focus on planning and reliability; uncomfortable with unstructured or unpredictable situations.

Low
Uncertainty
Avoidance

COOPERATIVE-COMPETITITVE

Cooperative: Emphasis on cooperation and nurturing behavior; high value placed on relationships and family.

Competitive: Emphasis on assertive behavior and competition; high value placed on work, task accomplishment, and achievement.

Moderate
Competitive

TIME ORIENTATION

Short-Term: Values immediate outcomes more than long-term benefits (success now).

Long-Term: Values long-term planning; willing to sacrifice short-term outcomes for long-term benefits (success later).

Short-Term
Time

CONTEXT

Low Context: Values direct communication; emphasis on explicit words.

High Context: Values indirect communication; emphasis on harmonic relationships and implicit understanding.

Moderate
Context

BEING-DOING

Being: Social commitments and task completion are equally important; diffuse boundaries between personal and work activities.

Doing: Task completion takes precedence over social commitments; clear separation of personal and work activities.

Moderate
Being/Doing

See Appendix B for comparison with other clusters.

*Significant variation within the cluster

All of the cultural value dimensions have relevance for understanding the Eastern European cluster. But understanding the key cultural value dimensions listed below is particularly important when interacting with cultural intelligence with people from the countries in this cluster.

Collectivist

For the most part, the cluster is Collectivist more than Individualist. But the moderate Collectivist orientation across Eastern Europe is primarily directed toward one's extended family, so it's unlikely someone will behave as much as a Collectivist in the work environment as they might if they're from an Asian or Arab culture. There is, however, a communal sense of looking out for each other. Many babushkas, or elderly Russian women, can't resist letting you know if you aren't dressed warmly enough, and they'll also be quick to help when you get caught in a bus door!

Power Distance

Similar to what we usually find with Collectivist cultures, the cluster tends toward higher Power Distance, though certainly not as much so as many Asian and African cultures. Within the extended family, there's an unspoken pecking order of who makes what calls, and a shared respect of those roles and the chain of command. Unlike many High Power Distance cultures, women have a greater degree of authority and status. Many of the families and clans have matriarchal histories, where the mother managed the day-to-day affairs on the homefront while the father was herding animals and preparing for the next move—or, in other cases, while the men were off fighting wars or sent off on work projects. So while the matryoshka icon is predominantly a Russian symbol, in a small way, it more broadly represents the matriarchal power structure that exists across this entire cluster as well.

Competitive

The cluster is moderately Competitive, something that is not too surprising given what was required for them to survive their battles with harsh terrain and weather, emperors, and other clans. Since other clans and tribes were viewed suspiciously at first—they were often competing for the same scarce resources—the people of this cluster developed a norm of tough resilience combined with curiosity and competitiveness toward newcomers. Allies were those who helped you win against the conquests of the emperors and Mother Nature.

People often complain about inferior customer service experienced at many businesses across this cluster. But, remember that, for many years, trading posts in this region that had products you wanted were doing you a favor by making it available, not vise versa. And throughout the Soviet era, there was often little incentive to provide good customer service to people.

Key Differences

During our journey around the world, we've continued to note differences that exist within each of the clusters. But the differences within Eastern Europe are far more stark than we've seen in the other clusters. The politics, language, economics, and religion all vary significantly from place to place within this cluster.

Despite the strong influence of the Orthodox Church in certain pockets of the cluster, there's a great deal of religious diversity. About 44 percent of the people living in this cluster identify themselves as Orthodox Christians. But 31 percent in the cluster identify as following a more Western Christian tradition. And there's a small but significant Muslim minority comprising about 16 percent of the population living in this cluster.

Nations like Russia, Slovenia, and Poland come from a Slavic origin. But Kazakhstan and Albania descend from a Turk-Muslim heritage, which results in very different cultural norms and practices. And there are numerous Hungarian groups spread across the cluster, people who originated as tribal groups in the Ural Mountains but now live all across the region. And the Mongols are yet another unique cultural group.

As we've continued to note on our journey around the world, there's value in seeing some of the historical connections shared across a cluster. Use these broad themes related to Eastern Europe as a starting point for digging deeper into understanding each place and the people you meet.

 ## Do's and Taboos

- English is widely spoken and understood across the region, but it's always good to learn a few words of greeting or how to say thanks in the specific language. This goes a long way toward respecting the unique heritage.

- One thing that is particularly offensive to people in many of the Eastern European cultures is to simply refer to them as being former soviet republics. They have a long history prior to that and expect you to know that.

- If you happen to be served something that you find unpalatable while dining at someone's house, your best bet is to eat it anyway. Serving guests the best and most expensive food is often a point of pride in many of these households, and you risk offending your host—or worse, hurting his or her feelings. Fortunately, bread is an almost constant accompaniment to any meal in Eastern Europe and Russia, so when the fish is too fishy or the caviar too salty you have something with which to smother the flavor.

- Expect to see very expressive, gregarious greetings among family and close   friends—including kissing several times on the cheeks or even on the lips. This is true between men and men as well as between women and women, and men and women; also expect that the greeting to an outsider will initially be the other extreme—aloof and cold until they become a trusted friend.

- Remember that not everyone in this cluster will fit these descriptions and there are huge differences among Eastern Europeans. Expect to find exceptions to the generalizations offered here.

Photo Credit: nosheepdesigns.com

5. LATIN EUROPE

EXAMPLES: France, French Canada, Italy, Latin Switzerland, Portugal, Spain, etc.

ICON: Fine Dining

Italians often say the quickest way to spot an American is to see someone who is twirling their spaghetti on their spoon. The French are known for gently introducing wine to their children at a young age. And a Spanish friend once asked me, "Why do Americans always keep one hand under the table while eating? What are they doing under there anyway?" Some of the finest cuisine in the world comes from the next cluster we're going to visit—Latin Europe. And Latin Europeans have very strong opinions about what and how to eat.

Seventy-five percent of French people still buy fresh bread daily from their local boulangerie. And to be called a boulangerie—the French word for bakery—the entire baking process must be done on site. Similar guidelines apply to bakeries across the rest of Latin Europe.

In recent years, a number of opportunistic entrepreneurs have attempted to mass-produce croissants, pizzas, and baguettes in France, causing tremendous controversy. In response, the government now regulates how foods can be sold and where, as a way of protecting the society from the ills of fast food.[1]

Ironically, McDonald's has been a huge success in Latin European cultures, but it didn't come easily. Marketing strategies have included decorating the store interiors with fake antique library shelves to make the dining areas look more Parisian, and McDonald's advertising campaigns in the region reassure people that, "It's okay to go to McDonald's once in awhile." When Latin Europeans do go to McDonald's, they rarely get their food to go or eat it on the fly; they eat in and linger over their food. McDonald's is most popular among Latin European teenagers who use it as a place to meet and hang out with friends.

Unless you go to Starbucks, you'll have a hard time finding a coffee "to go" in Paris, Madrid, or Lisbon. Coffee is meant to be enjoyed with a friend in the ambiance of a coffee shop, or after finishing your meal in a restaurant. Most people in the U.S. eat on the run and prefer a more laid-back approach to things like table manners.

The difference in eating protocol is just one factor that creates friction between many French and Americans. In general, Americans thrive on being informal and comfortable, so walking to work with a suit and tennis shoes might seem like common sense to a North American woman, while her French counterpart is likely to view it as very poor taste.

Overview

Latin Europe is sometimes referred to as the cradle of Europe. This is where the European miracle began, on the shores of the Mediterranean Sea. Europe is primarily the outcome of a triple heritage: Athens, Rome, and Jerusalem.

From Athens, Europe got Greek Rationalism, which led to the formal creation of science and philosophy. The Roman influence led to the organization of states and geopolitical systems built on the ideas of Roman Law. And from the Jews, the Latin Europeans adopted Judeo-Christianity, which they fused together with European art, science, philosophy, and government.

In the beginning, all of Western Europe was largely under the influence of the Roman Empire. But Northern Europe became increasingly disenchanted with the power of Rome and in particular, with the Church. So the northerners forged their own way apart from the southern region, and a huge divide formed between the two parts of Europe.

One of the most distinctive characteristics of the Latin European cluster is its paternalistic orientation. Sociologist Max Weber described paternalism as a parent, king, or feudal lord who provided protection in exchange for loyalty and obedience.[2] This is precisely the way the Caesars ruled the Roman Empire—"I'll take care of you but you have to give me your complete allegiance." This is certainly changing in the modern era across Latin Europe. People are rising up against governments and going into the streets to protest. But on the whole, some aspect of paternalism is far more prevalent in this cluster than other parts of Europe. For example, "gentlemanliness" is still highly valued across most of the cluster. Men are expected to hold the door for a woman, never be behind her when climbing the stairs, and pay the bill at the restaurant. Some business women in Paris prearrange to have the restaurant send the bill to her office so that she won't have to pay in the restaurant.

Gender equality has been slower to come to many Latin European companies and governments than other places around the world. This is beginning to change, but very slowly. For example, a 2010 study showed that women occupied about seven percent of Italy's corporate management positions, compared with an average of 30 to 35 percent in other developed nations. I suspect we'll continue to see changes in the role of women in Latin European companies and governments, but it's going to happen in ways that are consistent with the cultural norms of these ancient societies. Some women who are making the most in-roads describe having had fathers who really nurtured and supported them to realize their potential, which points to the paternalism that still exists, even among women who have broken through some of the barriers.[3]

While paternalism can be negative and destructive, the virtues behind it are based upon the idea that those with greater privilege, power, influence, and money should use their resources to take care of those who have not been given as much. The Latin Europe of the future is surely going to look different from the state-run, Latin Europe of the past. But the government will probably retain a more paternalistic slant in how it regulates, educates, and protects its citizens than you'll see in the rest of Europe.

Cultural Value Dimensions

The long history of certain European traditions won't go away quickly. For example, while fewer contemporary Latin Europeans might think of themselves as religiously devout, the values and ethos of the Roman Catholic Church still carry a lot of weight in how most Latin Europeans think and behave.

Cultural Value Definitions

	Latin Europe
INDIVIDUALISM-COLLECTIVISM *Individualism:* Individual goals and rights are more important than personal relationships. *Collectivism:* Personal relationships and benefiting the group are more important than individual goals.	Moderate Collectivist
POWER DISTANCE *Low Power Distance:* Status differences are of little importance; empowered decision-making is expected across all levels. *High Power Distance:* Status differences should shape social interactions; those with authority should make decisions.	Moderate Power Distance
UNCERTAINTY AVOIDANCE *Low Uncertainty Avoidance:* Focus on flexibility and adaptability; tolerant of unstructured and unpredictable situations. *High Uncertainty Avoidance:* Focus on planning and reliability; uncomfortable with unstructured or unpredictable situations.	High Uncertainty Avoidance
COOPERATIVE-COMPETITITVE *Cooperative:* Emphasis on cooperation and nurturing behavior; high value placed on relationships and family. *Competitive:* Emphasis on assertive behavior and competition; high value placed on work, task accomplishment, and achievement.	Moderate Cooperative
TIME ORIENTATION *Short-Term:* Values immediate outcomes more than long-term benefits (success now). *Long-Term:* Values long-term planning; willing to sacrifice short-term outcomes for long-term benefits (success later).	Moderate Time

CONTEXT *Low Context:* Values direct communication; emphasis on explicit words. *High Context:* Values indirect communication; emphasison harmonic relationships and implicit understanding.	Moderate Context
BEING-DOING *Being:* Social commitments and task completion are equally important; diffuse boundaries between personal and work activities. *Doing:* Task completion takes precedence over social commitments; clear separation of personal and work activities.	Moderate Being/Doing

See Appendix B for comparison with other clusters.

All of the cultural value dimensions have relevance for understanding the Latin European cluster. But the following are particularly significant for interacting with cultural intelligence when encountering people from the countries in this cluster.

Power Distance

Latin Europe scores moderate on the Power Distance continuum, but it's more attuned to status and hierarchy than any other "Western" cluster. While Latin European cultures certainly don't emphasize Power Distance the way an African culture does, chain of command and respect for authority is much more important in France and Italy than in Germany or Britain. And there's a collective deference to the authority and teachings of the Catholic Church.

Parents tend to speak more authoritatively to their children than do parents in most Western cultures today. And the governments in many of the Latin Europe countries are often expected to provide answers more frequently than what you would find in other Western contexts.

Uncertainty Avoidance

This cluster tends toward higher Uncertainty Avoidance. This might surprise you because we sometimes think of Italians and Spaniards as being spontaneous people who are comfortable with a great deal of chaos. But on the whole, Latin Europeans organize life around predictable structures and patterns, and prefer not to deviate from them; tradition and following the dominant norms are highly valued. Certainty isn't reached through schedules and policies, but from ascribing to the predominant religious and social norms.

Being

In contrast to most of their Western counterparts, the Latin European cultures are equally oriented toward Being and Doing. Latin Europeans define themselves by who they are more than what they've achieved. Your family name, your wealth status, your level of education ... these things are all important to Latin Europeans. And this emphasis on Being reinforces the importance of presenting a proper image of yourself, because what you wear says something about who you are.

In this cluster, there's a higher priority placed on enjoying life. This comes through in the eating customs described earlier. Eating is about both enjoying great food after a long day's work, and having extended conversation with family and friends. Lunch usually lasts a couple hours, and dinner may play out over three or more hours. Dinner begins at 8 p.m. in many of these countries, or even as late as 10 p.m. in many private homes or restaurants in Spain.

Despite the focus on Being, the Latin Europeans draw a very clear distinction between personal life and work life, something more characteristic of a Doing orientation. It wasn't easy, for instance, for EuroDisney management to convince its staff to come with their families to the amusement park. Family and work are kept separate.

Key Differences

French-Canadians are often put in this cluster because they have a great deal in common with Latin Europe. But one way the Quebecois French differ from the European French is in their eating habits. Many French are completely appalled at the eating habits of their Quebecois counterparts. And many people in Quebec loathe what they see as the uptight pretentions of the Parisians.

French and Italian-speaking Switzerland is also part of this cluster, but there are aspects of Germanic Switzerland that overshadow the Latin European norms. For example, Switzerland is very Low Power Distance, which is evident in how the country's presidency is structured. The presidency is a one-year duty that rotates among the seven members of the Federal Council, Switzerland's collective head-of-state. Many Swiss people—either Germanic or Latin—would be hard pressed to tell you who their current president is.

Not only are there significant differences within the Latin European cluster, there are also some stark differences within most of the countries included in the cluster. For example, the Basque people in Northern Spain are far more Doing-oriented and consumed with their work than most of the other people across Latin Europe. It's always valuable to pay attention to the cultural differences that exist within the same country, as well as recognizing the macro differences between countries in the cluster.

The biggest outlier in this cluster is Israel. Researchers include it in this cluster because of the similar Mediterranean terrain and the historical ties to the region, but, clearly, it's vastly different from Italy or Portugal. But, Rome dominated Israel for many years, just as it did the other countries in this cluster, and the Jewish people have had extensive influence across Latin Europe. The Vatican has retained long-standing holy ties to Bethlehem and Jerusalem, the cradle of Christianity. For several centuries, there have been strong Jewish communities in both France and Spain. And Israel has maintained significant social and business ties with Latin Europe. As with any country, if you're traveling to Israel or interacting extensively with someone from Israel, it's a good idea to learn some of the specifics of Israeli culture.

Do's and Taboos

- Dress appropriately before heading to a restaurant. Eating out, especially at a nice restaurant, is meant to be an event, and your attire will say something about whether you respect it as such. Don't be in a rush. The waiter or your fellow Latin European dining guests will quickly perceive rushed eating as rude. Eat everything with a utensil, including fruit and cheese. The exception is your bread or roll: You can use your hands, but break off a piece, eat it, and then break another.

- Being knowledgeable about a topic, even if it's an unusual hobby, will always be seen as an asset. A night out is not just about dressing up and going to dinner—it's also about demonstrating your refinement by sharing some knowledge.

- If you're eating with a business associate, don't discuss business right away. Wait until you're well into the meal, or even wait until coffee at the end. Eating is a time to enjoy the food and develop relationships, not to talk about work, especially if this is a new encounter.

- Paying for meals usually equals prestige. If you've been invited, the best way to respect your host is to say thank you and not put up a fight for the check. And then return the favor in the near future.

- When you go into a shop as an outsider, don't make demands such as, "I need some aspirin." Instead, given the paternalism of this region, it's far more effective to present yourself as a visitor in need and to ask for help. Try something like, "I wonder if you can help me? I'm trying to find the aspirin. Do you know where I might find that?"

- Remember that not everyone in this cluster will fit these descriptions! Enjoy the diversity that exists across Latin Europe.

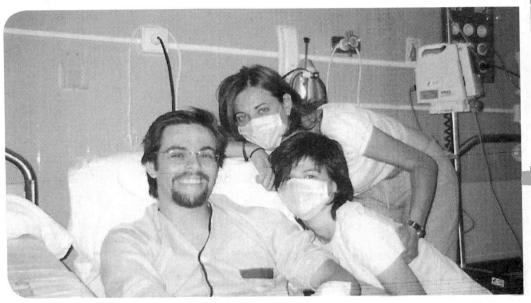

Photo Credit: Abel Pardo Lopez

6. LATIN AMERICA

EXAMPLES: Argentina, Brazil, Chile, Colombia, Costa Rica, Ecuador, Mexico, Venezuela, etc.

ICON: Family Member at Hospital

Most Latin American families wouldn't think about leaving their loved ones to be cared for exclusively by a professional. In fact, the custom in many Latin American hospitals is to leave the basic care for a patient to family members. Physicians are there to offer their expertise and do what only they can do; the bulk of the care is left to friends and family. From the Latin American perspective, it would be very unfortunate to have to entrust this kind of care to a clinical professional.

Several years ago, I was involved in a serious auto accident in Brazil. I was there with a group of high school students doing some service projects, and we decided to take a day off and rent dune buggies. I was riding in a dune buggy with three other guys and we were flying across the steep dunes that jutted out toward the ocean. All of a sudden, our driver lost track of where we were, took a sharp turn and we were suddenly airborne over a thirty-foot drop off.

The dune buggy crashed at the bottom. We were all conscious, but everyone was pretty banged up. Eventually, we ended up in a local hospital and the doctors discovered that I was bleeding internally. They had to operate to find out where the bleeding was coming from, and ended up removing my spleen, which had ruptured. For the next several days, I remained in this Brazilian hospital, but most of my care wasn't provided by the hospital itself. Instead, the North Americans with whom we'd been working in the community took shifts staying with me. They did many of the things that a nurse would typically do in hospitals back home: They took my temperature, helped me go to the bathroom, and helped me eat.

Initially, I assumed that outsiders performed these tasks because there weren't enough Brazilian nurses available to provide the care I needed. And, in fact, this is the explanation I was given by some of the North Americans who were there helping care for me. But I later learned that this may not have been the primary reason. There are certainly hospitals in South America that suffer from a shortage of nurses, but I was in a well-staffed, state-of-the-art Brazilian hospital. I didn't get the bulk of my basic care from nurses, because most Latin Americans wouldn't consider leaving the primary care of their loved ones to professionals.

Overview

The countries we'll encounter during this stop share a great deal of the cultural legacy found in Latin Europe. In fact, it has been observed that Latin America, culturally, is in many ways an extreme expression of many Latin European cultural traits—the paternalism, the role of government, and the explicit gender roles, to name a few. On the other hand, Latin America has also created its own unique norms, which partially minimizes the impact of certain Latin European values.

The most obvious differences between the Latin American and Latin European clusters are their geography and history. While Europe was being settled, the land we now know as Central and South America was populated by indigenous peoples who lived in groups isolated from each other. The local societies may have had some links between them in order to engage in commerce and trade, but for the most part, the indigenous tribes and communities were separated from one another by the region's dramatic terrain.

When Spain and Portugal colonized the region, they brought with them the language, culture, and institutions of Latin Europe. Most importantly, they brought Roman Catholicism, perhaps the biggest influence of Latin Europe on Latin America. Seventy-three percent of Latin Americans are Catholic, and 39 percent of Catholics worldwide are Latin American.[1]

In the decades since Latin America has become independent of European colonialism, many of these nations have struggled on so many fronts. Military dictatorships, U.S. domination, poverty, drugs, and revolutionary movements have created turmoil and strife across Latin America in the latter half of the 20th century—quite a contrast to the post-WWII resurgence that occurred in Europe. While Europe benefitted from the Marshall Plan and the presence of U.S. and NATO troops to help keep order, none of that existed in Latin America.

There's a growing attempt by Latin American countries to make a clean break with Latin European traditions, which many Latin Americans believe are behind their region's continuous cycle of economic and political turmoil. Leaving those traditions behind gives Latin Americans a sense of optimism about the future. Such optimism is difficult to find in Latin Europe, where overly optimistic people are often perceived as naïve. But, today, optimism is much more apparent on the streets of São Paulo, Mexico City, Santiago, La Paz, and Bogota.

Latin American countries were unquestionably shaped by their Spanish colonizers. Their predominant language, respect for family, custom of eating long meals together, and paternalism are primary ways in which the two clusters are similar. But on the whole, there's a more free-spirited, casual, optimistic outlook on life across Latin America than across Latin Europe. And the Latin Americans have a strong indigenous heritage that is still very evident in most countries.

Cultural Value Dimensions

Latin European colonization, Indigenous roots, and American idealism work together to create the Latin American cluster. On the one hand, most of the people in the cluster have socially liberal perspectives on the role of government and the importance of helping the poor. But they tend to be more socially conservative than many North Americans or Europeans when it comes to issues like homosexuality, abortion, and divorce.

Cultural Value Definitions

Latin America

INDIVIDUALISM-COLLECTIVISM

Individualism: Individual goals and rights are more important than personal relationships.

Collectivist*

Collectivism: Personal relationships and benefiting the group are more important than individual goals.

51

POWER DISTANCE
Low Power Distance: Status differences are of little importance; empowered decision-making is expected across all levels.

High Power Distance: Status differences should shape social interactions; those with authority should make decisions.

High
Power
Distance

UNCERTAINTY AVOIDANCE
Low Uncertainty Avoidance: Focus on flexibility and adaptability; tolerant of unstructured and unpredictable situations.

High Uncertainty Avoidance: Focus on planning and reliability; uncomfortable with unstructured or unpredictable situations.

High
Uncertainty
Avoidance

COOPERATIVE-COMPETITITVE
Cooperative: Emphasis on cooperation and nurturing behavior; high value placed on relationships and family.

Competitive: Emphasis on assertive behavior and competition; high value placed on work, task accomplishment, and achievement.

Moderate
Cooperative

TIME ORIENTATION
Short-Term: Values immediate outcomes more than long-term benefits (success now).

Long-Term: Values long-term planning; willing to sacrifice short-term outcomes for long-term benefits (success later).

Moderate
Time

CONTEXT
Low Context: Values direct communication; emphasis on explicit words.

High Context: Values indirect communication; emphasis on harmonic relationships and implicit understanding.

Moderate
High Context

BEING-DOING

Being: Social commitments and task completion are equally important; diffuse boundaries between personal and work activities.

Doing: Task completion takes precedence over social commitments; clear separation of personal and work activities.

Being

See Appendix B for comparison with other clusters.

*Significant variation within the cluster

All of the cultural value dimensions have relevance for understanding the Latin America cluster. But understanding the key cultural value dimensions listed below is particularly important when interacting with cultural intelligence with people from the countries in this cluster.

Collectivist

Latin American cultures are very Collectivist, but their collectivism is primarily oriented around the family. There's less devotion to institutional groups like workplaces or community organizations than what you might find in other Collectivist cultures. There's certainly some loyalty to the church and religious groups, but the primary source of identity is the family. To many Latin Americans, the family is everything. There's fairly low trust of those outside one's family network.

Power Distance

Similar to Latin Europe, the Latin American culture is paternalistic, and this comes through in the High Power Distance that exists across the region. Hierarchy and status is stronger across Latin American than in Latin Europe, and respect for hierarchy is most important within the family context.

Uncertainty Avoidance

Latin Americans are more averse to uncertainty and ambiguity than some other cultures. This seems like a contradiction with the laid-back, "que será será" Latino ethos. But change and uncertainty are avoided far more in Latin America than they are among the dominant cultures of North America.

However, the Latin American response to uncertainty is very different from that of the Germans or Japanese, who also have High Uncertainty Avoidance. Latinos are less likely to use laws, schedules, and policies to achieve certainty. Instead, they rely upon their religion and their family networks to attain certainty. Your best security lies in having someone you can trust to take care of you—the Church, your parents, or your friends at the hospital.

Being

The Latin American cluster is one of the most Being-oriented clusters in the world. There's a high priority placed on enjoying life. Work is not nearly as central to the typical Latino's identity as it is to those from more Doing-oriented cultures. And while Latin Americans aren't usually as concerned about eating etiquette and formalities as their Latin European counterparts are, the priority on sharing meals together is still very much the same.

One interesting difference among many Latin American cultures, as compared to Latin European ones, is that the main meal of the day has traditionally been the noon meal. Lunch was a long meal followed by a siesta during the hottest part of the day. The emergence of a global working culture and air conditioning has eliminated both the siesta and the long lunch from many working people's lives. But the heightened orientation toward Being is more evident in Latin American cultures than in most other places. And family trumps work. In fact, supervisors are often expected to attend the family functions of employees and to give special consideration to what happens to the family if an employee is fired.

Key Differences

As with all the clusters, each of the countries across Latin America has its own national culture. Brazil, for example, exhibits strong differences from the other Latin American countries because of its size (land mass, population, and economy), and as a result of being colonized by the Portuguese.

Argentina, Chile, and Uruguay more closely resemble Europe than do the other countries in this cluster. They're more individualistic than the Latin American norms. And then there are countries like Belize, where English is the predominant language and where the culture is more like that of the West Indies in the British Caribbean versus the dominant Latino culture. Guyana is also an English-speaking country, and Suriname is predominantly Dutch-speaking, which changes the way people in these countries think and behave.

It's important to note that there are rapid changes occurring among many of the young, urban Latin American populations. As in many other places around the world, Latin Americans are now connected by technology and attached to their mobile phones. Long conversations over dinner are becoming a thing of the past in some settings, and, for the first time, upper-class adult children are thinking about sending their aging parents to retirement centers.

The Latin American cluster has had increasing influence across North America. One of the fastest growing demographics in the U.S. is Latinos. It's important to note that Latinos in the U.S. are consistently frustrated by being talked about as if they're one unified cultural group; most often, they all get labeled as "Mexicans." But, Puerto Ricans are very different from Mexicans, and Venezuelans are different yet from Peruvians. Furthermore, many Latinos living in the U.S. have assimilated many cultural values from the Anglo cluster into their thinking and behavior, so they often have a strong combination of Anglo and Latin American values. As long as you remember these important differences when interacting with someone from this cluster, the kinds of generalizations used to describe it will be helpful.

✓ Do's and Taboos

- The American "come here" gesture is rarely used in Latin America unless you're trying to communicate a sexual solicitation. Instead, keep your hand "palm down" as you motion to "come here." (Similar to the motion you use to pet an animal.)

- Lighten up over schedules and time, both when you're waiting for someone or when you're the guest. Schedules and clocks just aren't as highly valued. It's expected that you would take time to greet and visit with a friend you encounter along the way, even if it means you might be late for another meeting.

- Don't ever underestimate the importance of building relationships. Relationships are the glue that makes life happen in this part of the world. Even if you're interacting with a customer service representative, treating them warmly will go a long way.

- Latin Americans are often much more comfortable with expressive communication, exaggerated gestures, and physical contact than many other cultures. And many Latinos have a smaller sense of personal space than do people from other cultures. It may be rude to step away from someone as they are stepping closer.

- Many people living across Central and South America consider themselves to be living in "America," so it's better to avoid using "America" to refer to the United States. And realize that there's some controversy as to whether the term "Latino" is welcomed or not, given that it's largely a label used in reference to the Latin colonizers.

- Remember that not everyone in this cluster will fit these descriptions! Be aware of differences among people in the Latin American world.

7. CONFUCIAN ASIA

EXAMPLES: China, Japan, Singapore, South Korea, Taiwan, etc.

ICON: Chopsticks

The widespread use of chopsticks is often associated with Confucius, one of the most influential philosophers and teachers who ever lived. Confucius believed that knives and forks represented aggression and violence, and should never be found at the table where you sit with friends and family; according to Confucius, food should be cut up in slaughterhouses and kitchens, rather than at the table. And so it's said that chopsticks were designed to not only move food from your table to your mouth, but to also reflect gentleness and benevolence—the main moral themes of Confucianism.

After dozens of trips to China, I've yet to see a fortune cookie at any restaurant I've ever visited there, nor have I ever seen a white Chinese takeout box. So, many of the stereotypical images we have about Confucian Asia may be challenged during our visit to this cluster.

Unlike fortune cookies and takeout cartons, chopsticks are a standard part of eating at Chinese and Japanese restaurants. There are some interesting superstitions and customs associated with chopsticks, including:

• If you find an uneven pair at your table in many Confucian cultures, it means you're going to miss a boat, plane, or train.

• Dropping chopsticks is believed to bring bad luck.

• Diners will sometimes cross their chopsticks at a dim sum restaurant to show the waiter that they're finished and ready to pay the bill. Or, sometimes the waiter will cross them to show that the bill has been settled.

• Leaving chopsticks so that they stick out of your food is a major faux pas, as it's done only at funerals when rice is put on the altar. And passing food from your chopsticks to someone else's is also frowned upon.

Whenever you see a pair of chopsticks, the most important thing to remember is what it symbolizes about Confucian Asia, the largest cluster in the world: This is a place where harmony and benevolence are the highest ideals.

Overview

Over the long haul of history, Confucian thought has likely carried as much clout as any other religion or philosophy. Confucianism is sometimes called "the religion of *li*," because *li* is an integral part of the Confucian way of thinking and behaving.[1]

Li literally means, "to arrange in order." If you've spent any time in Confucian cultures, traveled on Japanese or Korean airlines, or eaten at authentic Japanese, Korean, or Chinese restaurants, you almost definitely experienced *li*. *Li* means etiquette, customs, and manners; it's ceremony, courtesy, civility, and behaving with propriety. To the outsider, the Confucian culture can often feel intimidating because it appears there's a great deal of uptight formality and ritual. And indeed there is. But it isn't simply for the sake of being formal—it's all deeply symbolic. *Li* is represented by certain behaviors, which have been deemed appropriate by society.

Li might appear in the form of very formalized rituals—like the appropriate way to perform a wedding or a funeral—or it simply might be about how to behave at the dinner table. *Li* includes protocols about how children in all stages of life should respond to their parents: as young kids, as adults, even when their parents die. It also includes things like body language and appropriate dress for various occasions.

Conformity in and of itself isn't what's behind *li*. Instead, *li* is a means of expressing empathy and respect to one another—particularly within the family. Confucius' ultimate concern was cultivating benevolence and human kindness, which is the essence of a related Confucian priority: "*ren*." *Ren* is the inner harmony and peace-of-mind you experience when you've followed the order of *li*. It's a state of being, similar to what we often describe as being in a Zen state. *Ren* explains why *li* is so important. It's about fostering peace and harmony, so *ren* is the heart of relationships in Confucian Asia.

Li and *ren* are organized around five key relationships that govern most of life. This is the other most important thing to understand about Confucian culture. Once I understood this, it explained a whole lot of what I encounter when I interact with individuals from this part of the world.

1. **Ruler to Subject.** This relationship governs all the others. It's not about heartless command and control by the ruler. Instead, the people in charge should practice benevolent care, and subjects should remain loyal.

2. **Father to Son.** This is the most important family relationship, and it should be characterized by benevolence and provision from the father. In return, the son is to respond with filial piety and respect.

3. **Husband to Wife.** Next is the relationship between spouses. The husband should be caring and benevolent toward his wife, and the wife should listen and respect him.

4. **Elder Brother to Younger Brother.** The older brother should further extend the father's care to his younger sibling. And in the absence of the father, the elder brother assumes a fatherly role. He's expected to do so with gentleness. The younger brother/s should respond with humility and gratitude.

   Given the importance of an eldest son to Confucian culture, you can understand why it's such a big deal to families in these cultures to have a son, something that's a fifty-fifty chance in China, where the one-child policy is enforced.

5. **Elder Friend to Junior Friend.** This refers to the relationship between two friends. Elder friends are responsible for their juniors and, as a result, juniors should always defer to the older or more seasoned person in the relationship.

The key thing I'm always trying to determine when I'm interacting with someone from Confucian culture is which side of the relationship I'm on. Do they perceive me as being the one in the more senior, paternal role? Or am I perceived as the more junior, deferential person in the relationship? It's vital to understand this in order to interpret the kinds of things that may occur in your interactions with people from these cultures.

Cultural Value Dimensions

The priorities of harmony and gentleness run through the Confucian psyche. Psychologist Abraham Maslow is well known for his "hierarchy of needs" theory, which suggests people are motivated to fulfill basic needs before moving up to the most advanced need, self-actualization. It's been said that if Maslow had been Taiwanese, the top of the hierarchy would be social harmony. The priority of social harmony weaves through the everyday thinking and behavior of most people in Confucian Asia.

Cultural Value Definitions	Confucian Asia
INDIVIDUALISM-COLLECTIVISM *Individualism:* Individual goals and rights are more important than personal relationships. *Collectivism:* Personal relationships and benefiting the group are more important than individual goals.	Collectivist
POWER DISTANCE *Low Power Distance:* Status differences are of little importance; empowered decision-making is expected across all levels. *High Power Distance:* Status differences should shape social interactions; those with authority should make decisions.	Moderate Power Distance
UNCERTAINTY AVOIDANCE *Low Uncertainty Avoidance:* Focus on flexibility and adaptability; tolerant of unstructured and unpredictable situations. *High Uncertainty Avoidance:* Focus on planning and reliability; uncomfortable with unstructured or unpredictable situations.	Moderate* Uncertainty Avoidance

COOPERATIVE-COMPETITITVE	Moderate Cooperative
Cooperative: Emphasis on cooperation and nurturing behavior; high value placed on relationships and family.	
Competitive: Emphasis on assertive behavior and competition; high value placed on work, task accomplishment, and achievement.	
TIME ORIENTATION	Long-Term Time
Short-Term: Values immediate outcomes more than long-term benefits (success now).	
Long-Term: Values long-term planning; willing to sacrifice short-term outcomes for long-term benefits (success later).	
CONTEXT	High Context
Low Context: Values direct communication; emphasis on explicit words.	
High Context: Values indirect communication; emphasis on harmonic relationships and implicit understanding.	
BEING-DOING	Moderate* Being/Doing
Being: Social commitments and task completion are equally important; diffuse boundaries between personal and work activities.	
Doing: Task completion takes precedence over social commitments; clear separation of personal and work activities.	

See Appendix B for comparison with other clusters.

*Significant variation within the cluster

All of the cultural value dimensions have relevance for understanding the Confucian cluster, but the following are particularly significant for interacting with cultural intelligence when encountering people from the countries in this cluster.

Collectivist

The Confucian cluster is the most Collectivist one in the world. Confucian collectivism relates closely to the Chinese concept of "*guanxi*"—roughly translated as "connections." *Guanxi* is sometimes regarded by outsiders as Chinese xenophobia or cronyism, because it's built upon the idea of giving preferential treatment to insiders. Although *guanxi* can be abused, it is, at heart, simply a mode of relationship. And it's characterized by trust, mutual obligation, and most importantly, shared experience.

Guanxi may be seen, then, as the natural extension of the familial relationship system. In contrast, many Individualist cultures thrive on talking about relationships that have no strings attached. From a Confucian culture perspective, a relationship without strings attached is not a relationship. Friendship and familial relationships are built upon commitment and the expectation that there will be reciprocal commitment.

Long-Term Time Orientation

Most of the Confucian Asian countries score high on Long-Term Time Orientation. China, Hong Kong, Japan, and Korea sacrifice short-term benefits for long-term prosperity and success. It's not uncommon to read about a government initiative in Japan that will start being implemented ten years from now, something that would never fly in a short-term oriented culture. In fact, Sony is known for developing 100-year strategic plans. People in Confucian cultures are also less likely to spend money they don't have than people in short-term oriented cultures might do. Governments and businesses in this region tend to be cash-rich.

High Context

Communication is very High Context across Confucian Asia. People give as much attention to where individuals are seated, how they dress, and how they carry themselves as to what is actually said. Given the importance of *li*, the way you communicate verbally and nonverbally is more prescribed than it is in many other places. Most people in this cluster prefer to speak indirectly with peers, and they avoid confronting conflict head on. They pay a great deal of attention to the cues that come from the environment, more than to actual words spoken.

The High Context orientation of Confucian Asia is closely related to the high priority people put on saving face. Face is a heightened sense of one's own dignity and the dignity of others. You "give face" to people by making them feel good through generosity, kindness, and overall politeness. You "save face" by doing whatever you can to ensure your dignity isn't comprised, particularly in front of others. Many Confucian Asians go to great lengths to allow others to save face, particularly by not chastising them in front of others.

Key Differences

There are a few important ways that the Confucian cultures differ from each other. History is filled with examples of strife between the Chinese, Koreans, and Japanese. And Chinese and Japanese companies often have a very hard time working together. Part of this stems from long-standing prejudice and tension between the two countries, but it also stems from some differences along cultural values.

For example, China is more oriented toward Being and Japan is one of highest Doing cultures in the world. For a guest to pass on a social gathering in Japan may be less of an issue than it is in China, because there's a heightened priority placed on performance and working hard in Japan. In China, interacting with you socially (e.g. getting drunk late into the night) may be a tacit test of whether you can be considered trustworthy.

Another difference within the cluster is the variance in Uncertainty Avoidance, which is much higher in Singapore and Japan than in China. Minister Mentor Lee Kuan Yew, the "father" of Singapore, built the young country with an understanding of its extreme vulnerability. He instilled in people the realization that, as a tiny island country, Singapore was always just one step away from becoming obsolete. Lee Kuan Yew said, "We cannot view ourselves as being like Denmark or Luxembourg...We're in a turbulent region and we must always be prepared."[2] Reflecting that same High Uncertainty Avoidance, many Japanese companies forbid employees from ever discussing work outside of the office as a way to protect company secrets from outsiders—even work-related discussions at restaurants, on the elevator, or on public transit are forbidden by some Japanese companies.

Among the Chinese-dominant cultures, a variety of external factors have played a significant role in shaping the culture. Singapore developed its independence in a hostile environment and is deeply influenced by that today. Hong Kong's culture is shaped by the extended British colonization in the 20th century. Given the financial prosperity that ensued, the region adopted and retained many British business and management practices. And China itself was greatly influenced by the Cultural Revolution in the 1960s, when many people abandoned some of the more traditional Confucian behaviors and artifacts.

As always, use these clusters for a general idea of the cultural norms, and then dig into the specifics of the various cultures and individuals you encounter.

Do's and Taboos

- Pay careful attention to manners and etiquette in Confucian Asia. Sarcastic banter and swearing are unlikely to be good ways to break the ice or interact in either work or social settings unless you really know the people well. *Li* continues to be a guiding principle across Confucian Asia.

- If at all possible, eat with chopsticks. Today, it's not because people will view you as violent if you use a fork and knife, but you'll likely be seen as either an outsider who can't adapt or as an inflexible person who chooses not to adapt.

- Don't completely empty your plate. While many Western cultures view it as polite to clean your plate, the tradition in Confucian culture is that if you empty your plate, you will be given more food.

- Do whatever you can to promote harmony. Apologize whenever harmony is disrupted, and avoid gossiping and complaining openly about someone. Be careful of any behavior that has the potential to disrupt harmony.

- Spend a lot of time building trust before trying to develop a formal business relationship.

- Business cards or name cards are very important. Be sure to bring enough with you when you travel to these regions. Stand when giving and receiving the cards, take a moment to study the ones you receive, and try to say the individual's name and role. Place it on the table in front of you and don't write on it.

- Remember that not everyone in this cluster will fit these descriptions! Be prepared to encounter exceptions.

8. SOUTHERN ASIA

EXAMPLES: India, Indonesia, Malaysia, Philippines, Thailand, etc.

ICON: Curry

Curry is a widely used term to refer to a variety of dishes that typically come from the next cluster on our journey. The common feature among curried dishes is a mixture of spices and herbs, with hot chilies usually included. A Thai curry (red, green, or yellow) tastes very different from a South Indian curry, and a Khmer curry is different from a Malay one. The various curries reflect the regional, religious, and family differences across the region. The Southern Asian cluster is a place that has historically been rich in diversity where people from vastly different religions and cultures, speaking diverse languages, and following different traditions have co-existed together harmoniously for many centuries.

One time an Indian woman who moved to the U.S. told me how much she loved the traditional American Thanksgiving dinner because of its simplicity. I remember thinking, *Simple?! How can you call Thanksgiving dinner simple?* Yet compared to an Indian meal, which may sometimes require several days of grinding spices, making yogurts, and preparing dishes, the traditional Thanksgiving dinners eaten in the U.S. and Canada are indeed relatively simple.

If you come to my house and we have a variety of dishes on the table, I don't want you to feel obligated to eat everything. Granted, I'll probably feel bad if you don't eat anything we've prepared. But if you don't like broccoli, by all means don't choke it down just to make me feel good.

But to pass on eating a dish prepared for you during our visit to Southern Asia could be a great offense. The spices used may have been grown in the family garden for decades, or even centuries. And the kind of meal typically served to a guest probably took hours, perhaps days to prepare. Food is an extension of one's self and one's family homestead. You'll also find that many Southern Asians prefer to get up close and personal with their food by eating it with their hands. As one Indian friend told me, "Eating with a knife and spoon is like making love through an interpreter." Southern Asians love to immerse themselves in their flavorful foods.

Overview

The cultures across Southern Asia abound with diversity in every sense of the word. The thing that's tricky about understanding this cluster is that its unifying theme is its flavorful diversity. So to outsiders, this cluster can appear rather disjointed and in turmoil. But, the most distinct feature of the region is the rather peaceful and interactive co-existence of such diverse cultures over long periods of time. Now, obviously there are exceptions. For example, the relationship between India and Pakistan is not exactly a picture of peaceful coexistence. And there have been longstanding tensions in various pockets, such as between the Chinese and Malays in Malaysia, or between Christians and Muslims in the Philippines. But for the most part, the people of this region have coexisted peacefully for long periods of time despite their differences.

Those differences can be stark. Across India, for example, you frequently find Islamic mosques next to Hindu temples, and Buddhist pagodas next to Christian churches and Sikh gurudwaras. These diverse forms of faith in such densely populated places seem irreconcilable, yet they co-exist peaceably throughout most of Southern Asia.

You'll also find a colorful curry of ethnic cultural influences across the cluster. There's a pervasive Arab influence in many of these nations and an even stronger Chinese presence; there are Portuguese, Dutch, and British influences across various pockets in the region. And you'll even find strong Spanish and U.S. influences in the Philippines. This cluster has been unusually adept at assimilating modern and external influences with their own indigenous cultures. Just take a look at how India has assimilated some very British practices while still remaining very thoroughly Indian.

The diversity of cultures and religions that exists within this cluster is also present within India itself. There are 10,000 different languages spoken across the country. Hindi is the principal official language of India, with English an official secondary language. The government formally recognizes 22 different languages. Indonesia features the same kind of diversity, with more than 700 living languages, and a mix of Muslims, Christians, and Hindus; a similar diversity exists in Malaysia.

Indian culture is no easy composite of styles and values. In the matter of cuisine, you have big differences between northern and southern foods, and the peppery hot food of Andhra and the largely coconut-based cuisine of coastal Kerala. Likewise, when it comes to architecture, you have the great temple cities of the south and the planned out city of Chandigarh in the north. There's the intricate architecture of Delhi, and the roadside shrines of Gujarat. But what unites the Indian people most of all is a mild, calm spirit that's in stark contrast to the aggressive zeal they've often experienced at the hands of their conquerors and colonizers. I'm not referring so much to their personality—Indians are quite often outgoing and assertive—but the Indian society as a whole has a calm transcendence to it, mirroring what's found across the Southern Asian cluster as a whole.

Throughout this cluster, service is a value most people grow up with. Guests are revered and pampered. In most cases, it's deemed perfectly okay if guests arrive unannounced, particularly if they have a close relationship with the host; in many Western cultures, this would be viewed as an imposition. And while Western businesses devote significant resources to training staff to provide good customer service, this kind of training isn't as necessary in Southern Asia—it's a value most people here have grown up with. Many Southern Asians are frustrated when multinationals insist on teaching them something that is so obvious and innate to their cultural practices.

Cultural Value Dimensions

Given the vast diversity across the Southern Asia cluster, it's difficult to identify shared cultural values. The respect for diversity itself is a core value. But there are a few patterns that dominate most of the cultures across this cluster.

Cultural Value Definitions	Southern Asia
INDIVIDUALISM-COLLECTIVISM *Individualism:* Individual goals and rights are more important than personal relationships. *Collectivism:* Personal relationships and benefiting the group are more important than individual goals.	Collectivist
POWER DISTANCE *Low Power Distance:* Status differences are of little importance; empowered decision-making is expected across all levels. *High Power Distance:* Status differences should shape social interactions; those with authority should make decisions.	High Power Distance
UNCERTAINTY AVOIDANCE *Low Uncertainty Avoidance:* Focus on flexibility and adaptability; tolerant of unstructured and unpredictable situations. *High Uncertainty Avoidance:* Focus on planning and reliability; uncomfortable with unstructured or unpredictable situations.	Moderate Uncertainty Avoidance
COOPERATIVE-COMPETITITVE *Cooperative:* Emphasis on cooperation and nurturing behavior; high value placed on relationships and family. *Competitive:* Emphasis on assertive behavior and competition; high value placed on work, task accomplishment, and achievement.	Moderate Cooperative
TIME ORIENTATION *Short-Term:* Values immediate outcomes more than long-term benefits (success now). *Long-Term:* Values long-term planning; willing to sacrifice short-term outcomes for long-term benefits (success later).	Moderate Time

CONTEXT *Low Context:* Values direct communication; emphasis on explicit words. *High Context:* Values indirect communication; emphasis on harmonic relationships and implicit understanding.	High Context
BEING-DOING *Being:* Social commitments and task completion are equally important; diffuse boundaries between personal and work activities. *Doing:* Task completion takes precedence over social commitments; clear separation of personal and work activities.	Moderate* Being/Doing

See Appendix B for comparison with other clusters.

*Significant variation within the cluster

All of the cultural value dimensions have relevance for understanding the Southern Asian cluster, but the following are particularly significant for interacting with cultural intelligence when encountering the cultures from this cluster.

Collectivist

Southern Asia is very Collectivist, but in a way that's different from Confucian Asia. Family is an important source of one's collective identity, just as is true in Confucian Asia, but there's a greater ease with Individualism here than there is in Confucian Asia. There's less pressure to conform to your in-group's expectations, and more freedom to pursue individual dreams.

Having respect and consideration for one's parents is still extremely important. But, particularly in countries like Thailand, Laos, and Cambodia, individuals are freer to move to their own drumbeat than in other parts of Asia. But a Southern Asian still develops his or her identify first and foremost in connection to his or her in-group—typically the extended family.

Power Distance

The Power Distance in this cluster is very high. In nearly all of the countries in this cluster, you can clearly see a stratification of people according to their status and roles. There are prescribed roles for people according to their caste, or status, and overlooking those norms is met with great resistance.

Saving face is a very important consideration in this cluster as well. Part of this stems from the desire to ensure that respect is extended to people regardless of their religious or cultural background, but it's also related to the importance of respecting people according to their status. Using formal titles for people of "higher status" and considering where people should be seated around a table are priorities that have greater importance to many of the people in these cultures.

Uncertainty Avoidance

A frequent Thai expression is, "Mai pen rai," which means "No worries" or "Never mind about that." This captures the very laid back, moderate level of Uncertainty Avoidance that exists among many of the cultures in this cluster. Most of the countries across the cluster have worked hard to minimize the number of rules and laws that infringe upon people's diverse perspectives in order to promote the curried, peaceful co-existence of so many different faiths and backgrounds.

Key Differences

As one of the largest clusters in the world, with more than one billion people in India alone, there are some important differences to bear in mind as you travel across the region. Countries like Thailand, Cambodia, and Laos are more oriented toward Being; the priority upon enjoying life and improving one's well-being is evidenced by the prevalence of things like massage, meditation, and festivals. India, on the other hand, has a much higher Doing orientation. For example, many Indian companies expect anyone who has a smart phone to be available 24/7 if the company needs to reach them.

Thailand has a much higher acceptance of people deviating from preferred norms than do places like India and Pakistan. Thailand, by the way, is also very proud of the fact that it's never been colonized; the Thai people make it a point to reference that difference often.

Similar to what we find in many other clusters, the younger generation in Southern Asia is showing some differences in their values. Young people today interact with their parents differently than the previous generation did—but, this is still relative. A 25-year-old Malay guy might seem much less concerned about hierarchy and respect for status than his father would; but if he follows the norms for Southern Asia, he'll still seem to have much higher Power Distance than a "typical" 25-year-old from the Nordic cluster will.

Do's and Taboos

- Be conscious of eating preferences throughout the region. Many within the Southern Asian cluster are vegetarian, or they don't eat beef or pork; some abstain from alcohol, too. You don't have to keep track of each person's precise dietary restrictions, but simply asking the question goes a long way. If you're choosing a restaurant for a group of friends, look for one that accommodates the varied eating preferences that might be among your friends.

- Just because this cluster is very tolerant doesn't mean they welcome talking about religious and cultural differences. One of the ways the cluster has accomplished living together peacefully is choosing to avoid much discussion about religious differences. Now, there are exceptions to this. For example, foreign military personnel and civilian aid workers are often taught to avoid discussing religion with Afghans at all cost. Yet some Afghans are very interested in discussing religion and hearing visitors' opinions on it. As always, tread carefully and let them take the lead on a topic like this. And use the utmost respect as you talk about any religion.

- Most of the places across this cluster are densely populated and hence crowded. As a result, be prepared for small amounts of interpersonal space when spending time here.

- The cultures across this cluster are very different from the cultures most familiar to many travelers. Take It in in bite-size chunks or you may get overwhelmed. People unfamiliar with an Indian market or Filipino bus are often overstimulated, but if taken in small doses you will enjoy the abundance of diversity that exists.

- Remember how important the food is to the various cultures. If at all possible, try whatever you're given and remember your nonverbals are being watched. Southern Asians are very High Context, so they're paying attention to more than just what you say.

- Remember that not everyone in this cluster will fit these descriptions! Be ready for exceptions, particularly as you meet Southern Asians in other places around the world.

Photo Credit: Cindy Soroka

9. SUB-SAHARAN AFRICA

EXAMPLES: Ghana, Kenya, Namibia, Nigeria, Zambia, Zimbabwe, etc.

ICON: Ubuntu

As you travel across our next cluster, you'll encounter the pervasive influence of Ubuntu—an age-old African ideal that says, "I am what I am because of who we all are." Whether observing ancient tribal customs in rural regions, political rhetoric, or business practices across major urban areas, you'll see a heavy emphasis on interconnectedness across the Sub-Saharan Africa cluster. This includes interconnectedness with each other, with society, with the spiritual realm, and with nature. Ubuntu understands that when you do good, it spreads out for all of humanity; when you don't, it throws off the whole natural system. You can even see a couple of military police, patrolling an area, walking hand in hand—Ubuntu.

There's a widely shared story about an anthropologist who proposed a game to a group of kids in an African tribe. He put a basket full of fruit under a tree and told them, "Whoever gets there first will win the sweet fruits." They all got ready, and he said, "Go!" But, when he told them to run, they all took each other's hands and ran together. When they got to the tree, they sat together and all enjoyed the fruit.

When the anthropologist asked them why they ran together instead of seeing if they could get the prize all for themselves, they replied, "Ubuntu, Ubuntu," meaning, "I am because we are." Ubuntu means reciprocity and it's built into everything naturally. It's the virtue of symbiosis and believing that interdependence flows through every relationship. Ubuntu says your best way to support and promote reciprocity is to suppress your self-interest and to live on behalf of your family and tribe.

At the crux of Ubuntu is your family. There's no cluster that makes more of the extended, kinship model of family than does the Sub-Saharan Africa cluster. When you think of an African family you should think more of a kinship model of family, the multi-layered, extended family, not simply a nuclear family.

Ubuntu further extends to other social groups—traditionally the tribe and, today, it may also extend to one's schoolmates, neighborhood, work affiliations, or religious memberships. Many communities across Sub-Saharan Africa go to great lengths to be in tune with each other, with nature, and with the spiritual realm. There are a number of traditional leadership roles established to reflect these priorities, including kings and queens, rain makers, and witch doctors. Many of these roles can still be found among tribal groups across the cluster today. You're less likely to find them in urban settings, but it's certainly possible. And at the very least, you'll notice that a consciousness exists about the interconnectedness between humanity, nature, and the transcendent realm, much more so than you'll see in most other places.

Overview

When outsiders think of Africa, they often conjure up images of tribal people, slavery, or corruption. As with most stereotypes, there's a kernel of truth in most of these ideas, but most information about Africa is very skewed. Part of what you'll discover as we journey through Africa is that it's a place full of contradictions, complexity, and contrasts.

While disease, poverty, and illiteracy are still huge problems across Africa, one BBC poll found that 90 percent of Africans surveyed are proud to be African and consider themselves to be successful and thriving. Not everyone in Africa is starving and wishing they could get off the continent. Companies like IBM, Google, Turkish Airlines, Microsoft, and Harley Davidson are just a few of the multinational businesses that are rapidly expanding their presence in Sub-Saharan Africa.

Most of the cultures across Africa have long, storied histories. In fact, it's widely believed to be the place where human civilization began.

The early development of things like iron tools led to the establishment of sophisticated settlements like the kingdom of Ghana in West Africa. Hundreds of years ago, Ghana was a large city with many fine houses, buildings, and markets, filled with rich palm trees and surrounded by henna plantations.

From the 8th century onward, Arab trading penetrated Sub-Saharan Africa. The Arabs traded oil, lamps, and pottery for ivory, ebony, gold, and slaves. And they also brought Islam with them.

The Portuguese were the first Europeans to move into this region, and they started slave trade; they were quickly crowded out by the British, Belgians, French, and Germans. The presence of all these European colonizers left a huge imprint of Christianity and Western Civilization on the continent.

Today, the fastest growing population among Christians worldwide is in Africa. For every Western Christian missionary that goes to Nigeria, Nigeria sends out five missionaries of its own to various places around the world. But Christianity in Africa looks very different than it does in North America and Europe. There's an indigenous approach to Christianity that at times looks as much like the tribal religions as It does Western Christianity. Similar developments are occurring among African Muslims.

Africa is a deeply religious place. One of the things you may notice during our visit to this cluster is the abundance of religious references that permeate many African towns and cities. For example, taxis may paint scriptural references across their windows, and bakeries may be named things like "The Bread of Life Bakery." I saw my all-time favorite business name in Accra, Ghana, where the local hairdressing shop was called "All Things are Possible Beauty Salon."

One time I had a Sudanese student who missed the beginning of the semester because he was back in Sudan trying to secure his engagement to his fiancée by coming up with 40 cattle to pay her father. Given that he was studying in the U.S., it was expected that he should be able to come up with a significant bride price for his fiancée's family, and there was really no way out of it. Furthermore, he had to ensure that the cattle were cared for in a very careful manner, since he was offering them as his bride price for the woman who would connect the family to its ancestral roots and future generations.

Because of Ubuntu, it's nearly impossible for an African to move abroad to North America, Europe, or Asia and not continue to send money back home. The priority and expectation of interconnectedness continues, even if you leave the continent. Often times, individuals might be barely getting by, making minimum wage to support themselves living in Atlanta or Brussels, but there's still an expectation that they will send some of the money they're earning back home to their extended family.

Life for most Africans is very holistic. They live with a profound sense that a spiritual force and energy permeates the universe, and day-to-day choices and interactions need to reflect that understanding.

Cultural Value Dimensions

The tribal heritage of Africa combined with the painful colonization it experienced continues to shape the thinking and behavior of the individuals living across this region. The cluster is a paradox of defeat and survival, tribal and urban, agricultural and industrial.

Cultural Value Definitions	Sub-Saharan Africa
INDIVIDUALISM-COLLECTIVISM *Individualism:* Individual goals and rights are more important than personal relationships. *Collectivism:* Personal relationships and benefiting the group are more important than individual goals.	Collectivist
POWER DISTANCE *Low Power Distance:* Status differences are of little importance; empowered decision-making is expected across all levels. *High Power Distance:* Status differences should shape social interactions; those with authority should make decisions.	Moderate Power Distance
UNCERTAINTY AVOIDANCE *Low Uncertainty Avoidance:* Focus on flexibility and adaptability; tolerant of unstructured and unpredictable situations. *High Uncertainty Avoidance:* Focus on planning and reliability; uncomfortable with unstructured or unpredictable situations.	Moderate Uncertainty Avoidance
COOPERATIVE-COMPETITITVE *Cooperative:* Emphasis on cooperation and nurturing behavior; high value placed on relationships and family. *Competitive:* Emphasis on assertive behavior and competition; high value placed on work, task accomplishment, and achievement.	Cooperative
TIME ORIENTATION *Short-Term:* Values immediate outcomes more than long-term benefits (success now). *Long-Term:* Values long-term planning; willing to sacrifice short-term outcomes for long-term benefits (success later).	Short-Term Time

CONTEXT *Low Context:* Values direct communication; emphasis on explicit words. *High Context:* Values indirect communication; emphasis on harmonic relationships and implicit understanding.	High Context
BEING-DOING *Being:* Social commitments and task completion are equally important; diffuse boundaries between personal and work activities. *Doing:* Task completion takes precedence over social commitments; clear separation of personal and work activities.	Being
See Appendix B for comparison with other clusters.	

All of the cultural value dimensions have relevance for understanding the Sub-Saharan Africa cluster, but the following are particularly significant for interacting with cultural intelligence when encountering people from the countries in this cluster.

Collectivist

Africa is very Collectivist, just like most of the clusters in the world. But for the Sub-Saharan African cluster, collectivism is so vital to their psyche that it's difficult to conceive of being a person apart from the larger group.

One time I was at a conference in Uganda where each guest was given his own hotel room. Nonetheless, most of the African delegates bunked together, four or five people to a room. When I asked one Ugandan man about it he said, "I've never spent a night alone in my entire life. The very thought of it frightens me." For most Africans, collectivism is not simply a way you think about your identity; it signifies that relationships are the only way you exist. This is Ubuntu at work.

Cooperative

Ubuntu means that cooperation and interdependence are vitally important, so the Sub-Saharan Africa cluster is most definitely oriented toward the Cooperative side of the Cooperative-Competitive value dimension. Businesses that go into Africa presenting a value proposition by appealing to competitive instincts are unlikely to be successful. Success and results are valued, but the way to get there is through cooperation.

International businesses that want to develop a presence in Africa are often expected to give money to a village project or some other aid and development initiative. And given the spiritual orientation across many of

77

the countries in this cluster, there will be an expectation for outsiders to at least respect the importance of the human-divine interdependence.

Being

Finally, who you are is far more important from the African perspective than what you do. Individuals typically identify themselves in light of their extended families, and there isn't the same concern for efficiency and achievement among many of the countries in this cluster as there is elsewhere in the world. Africans often say to Westerners: "You have the watches. We have the time." There's a much more relaxed, laid-back approach to life across this cluster than there is in the Western world.

This laid-back approach is beginning to change as more African countries, leaders, and businesses want to play a more global role. Foreign investment in Africa is up significantly compared to a few years ago. IBM recently opened up a massive office in Senegal. Orange, a French cell-phone company, and Baidu, China's answer to Google, introduced a jointly branded smartphone browser in Africa in early 2013. And many Africans themselves are developing multinational companies that are beginning to compete with other global enterprises, both inside and outside the continent. As a result, there's an increase in the Doing and Competitive inclination found among many individuals across the cluster. But the predominant orientation in the Sub-Saharan African mind is overwhelmingly toward Being.

Key Differences

Even though Africa often gets referred to as if it were one country, each African country and the thousands of tribal groups across the continent have customs that are very unique to them. And despite the emphasis upon Ubuntu, there's a great deal of inter-ethnic, racial, and tribal conflict throughout the cluster. As with most Collectivist societies, commitment and loyalty is to one's own in-group.

At one level, it can seem that the only thing the Sub-Saharan African cultures have in common is the dark experience of colonization and enslavement. But that experience is part of what unites the many different cultures across the cluster. There's a driving sense of survival that is consistent to the cluster. Tribal people and farmers have always had to compete for scarce land and water resources, and that continues to this day. Meanwhile, the urban populations across the cluster are striving to make their own mark on the global scene of business and economics.

The various colonizers account for some of the differences experienced across the cluster, including influences from Arab, Dutch, British, French, and Portuguese cultures. And within each country there are also strong tribal differences. Other differences created by outside influences have been a source of great conflict, such as the battles between the Hutu and Tutsi groups in Rwanda or the Americos (repatriated slaves) and indigenous people in Liberia.

Perhaps the biggest outlier in this cluster is South Africa. In fact, part of South Africa is grouped in the Anglo cluster because of the predominance of British culture, which is seen particularly in the business culture of South Africa. The Dutch Afrikaans culture also plays a significant role in South Africa, as does the Indian culture. Cities like Capetown and Johannesburg are highly developed places and look more like Western metropolitan areas than typical African ones. But simply venture into a nearby township or go beneath the surface of the global chains in these cities and you'll find some thoroughly African aspects to South African people and organizations.

The Sub-Saharan African culture has experienced less homogenization across the cluster than have most of the other clusters. But one of the important things to remember as you encounter people and places across Sub-Saharan Africa is that a great deal of traditional, tribal identity exists everywhere you go.

Do's and Taboos

- Small talk and asking about the health and well being of other people's family is especially important. Don't jump right to business. Allow people to take time to introduce themselves in light of their extended families. They see it as very relevant.

- Dress modestly. Africa continues to be a very conservative culture and modesty is strongly valued.

- Be very careful how you ask about a loved one who has passed away. Let them take the lead on if and how they refer to it; while respect and honor are   always appropriate with this kind of situation, they are particularly important to this culture. Even if an African refers to someone who died several years ago, there remains a great deal of superstition associated with death.

- If you travel there, be street smart as you would anywhere you go. Look confident and don't make yourself vulnerable by being alone in a place where you aren't sure about the safety. But if you have the desire to explore this ancient, fascinating place—by all means go.

- Don't expect that everyone is living in a tribal village and spotting lions out their backdoor, but neither should you disregard the influence of many ancient customs.

- Remember that not all Africans will fit these descriptions! Look for the vast differences that exist across this fascinating continent.

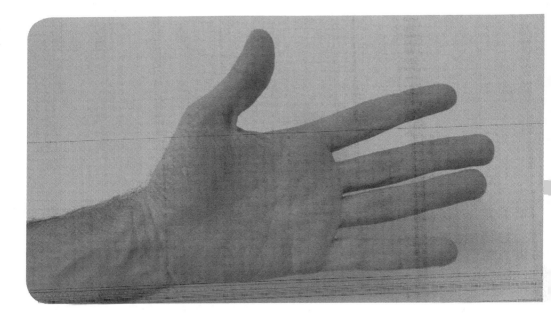

10. ARAB

EXAMPLES: Bahrain, Egypt, Jordan, Kuwait, Saudi Arabia, Tunisia, U.A.E, etc.

ICON: Left Hand

Left-handed people may have a bit harder time visiting our last cultural cluster than right-handed people will. According to Islam, the left hand is considered unclean and is reserved for personal hygiene. Arabs traditionally use the right hand for all public functions, including shaking hands, eating, drinking, and passing objects to another person. Traditionally, parents try to teach their children to be right handed, regardless of their natural dexterity. The left hand is used to clean yourself in the bathroom. This custom is true in other places around the world, too—including certain parts of Africa and Asia—but its significance is iconic in the Arab cluster.

I recently did some work with the Saudi government. They invited me to help them consider how they could improve their effectiveness in attracting and retaining foreign talent. They brought me over on their national airline, Saudia, and my experience with Saudi culture began immediately.

Before takeoff from Washington, D.C., we were asked to remain silent during the prayers to Allah, and at various times throughout the flight, people were in designated areas kneeling on their prayer mats. There was no alcohol served on the flight, and available magazines had all been pre-censored. As I read through a copy of *Time Magazine*, I discovered that pieces of white tape had been placed over pictures of scantily clothed women and certain articles had been ripped out. I picked up a couple other copies of the same issue on the plane and, sure enough, it was the same thing in every copy.

Religion plays a role in the cultural fabric of many of the ten clusters, but its influence is most evident when looking at the role of Islam upon the Arab cluster, our final stop in our worldwide tour. Saudi Arabia is the extreme example of this influence, but across the cluster as a whole, there's a tighter definition for how people should and should not behave than what you see in other cultural clusters.

Overview

People around the globe have many misconceptions about what it means to be Arab, including everything from a lack of understanding of the differing roles of men and women to the influence of Arab oil in the world. The 21st century needs global leaders who understand the Arab cluster, and how to effectively and respectfully engage with people from this ancient region.

On the whole, the people in the Arab cluster are a vibrant group who love family, participate in a wide variety of occupations, love to travel, and have a strong sense of loyalty to their cultural identity. To be an Arab is a cultural identity more than an ethnic heritage. It's similar to how North Americans think of themselves, but that doesn't entirely capture it either. A key factor in defining cultural identity in this cluster is usually associated with speaking Arabic as a first language. In fact, the Arabic language is so strongly identified with what it means to be an Arab that speaking Arabic as your first language and being considered an Arab are pretty much synonymous.

Being an Arab also typically means having family ties that originate in this region. The Arab cluster stretches from Morocco, across North Africa, and on to the Persian Gulf. And the individuals who are considered part of this cluster descend from the early tribes that occupied the Arabian Peninsula.

Being Arab doesn't necessarily mean you're Muslim. In fact, the majority of Muslims do not live in the Arab cluster. There are also Jews, Christians, and agnostics who live in the region. But there's no question, Islam has a ubiquitous influence on the countries in this cluster. Even those Arabs who aren't religiously devout are usually influenced by some of the Islamic ideals and tenets, and often refer to themselves as "cultural Muslims." Given the importance of Islam to this cluster, it's helpful to have a fundamental understanding of Islam and its five pillars of faith.[1]

Islam means complete submission to God. This is central to everything else in Islam. Obedience to Allah covers every facet of a person's life, from personal hygiene to business transactions. Muslims believe that all prophets prior to Muhammad were preaching the same message, therefore most Muslims have high regard for all religions.

1. **Shahadah.** This is the first and most important pillar of Islam. It means to "testify" that there is only One God and that Muhammad is His messenger. To "say the Shahadah" is a prerequisite to becoming a Muslim, and it's considered a declaration of your faith.

    Muslims believe that the driving response to Shahadah should be one of submission to God, to accept God's law and will for your life. Consequently, pluralism and allowing people to arrive at their own conclusions often runs in direct conflict with this core tenet of Islam. You'll frequently hear Muslims insert the word "Inshallah" as they speak, an Arabic word for "if God wills."

2. **Salat/Prayer.** You can't travel to this part of the world without being continually reminded of prayer. The call to prayer happens five times a day, 365 days a year in the Arab world, and Muslims have heeded this call to prayer for more than a millennium. The prayer ritual includes cleansing the body by washing the face, head, arms, and feet, kneeling toward Mecca, and, when possible, visiting the local mosque. The prayer consists of reading chapters from the Quran, which is in Arabic. In any other language, it is considered a translation, not the word of God.

    Fridays are the day of worship in Arab countries. This means the weekend in this part of the world includes Friday—so the weekend is Thursday/Friday or Friday/Saturday, depending upon the specific country involved.

3. **Zakat/Alms.** Muslims believe that everything belongs to God, and that wealth is only entrusted to humans for a time. The word zakat means purification. A person's possessions are purified by setting aside a portion of them for those in need and for society in general. Generosity and sharing with others are very strongly held values across the Arab cluster. And Muslims follow the Koranic principle of not charging interest on loans.

4. **Sawm/Fasting.** Every year during Ramadan, a month-long sacred holiday, all Muslims fast from dawn until sundown, abstaining from food, drink, sex, and impure thoughts. Developing self-discipline and resisting your vices is a predominant emphasis

in Islam. If you travel to the Middle East during Ramadan, you may have a hard time finding a restaurant open during the day and you should avoid eating in public during daylight hours.

5. **Hajj/Pilgrimage.** All devout Muslims strive to get to Mecca at least once during their lifetime. This is only an obligation for those who are physically and financially able to do so, but over two million people travel to Mecca each year from every corner of the globe, which provides a unique opportunity for those of different nations to meet one another.

The hijab, or the traditional head covering worn by Arab women, has generated a great deal of controversy across the world. On the one hand, many Westerners view the veil as oppressive and restrictive—and some Arab women agree with that viewpoint. But there are other Arab women who talk about the freedom they feel by wearing the hijab. They say it keeps them from being objectified solely based upon their appearance. Also, in Islam, the hair is the crown of a woman's beauty, and many Arab women prefer to preserve their beauty for their husbands and families alone. Some Islamic women suggest that asking them to walk outside their home without the hijab feels comparable to asking a Westerner to walk outside their house in their underwear. It really is that big of a deal to many Arab women.

Cultural Value Dimensions

The Arab cluster scores similar to many other clusters in several of its cultural values, but religion plays a much bigger role in how these values developed in the first place. Of course, the heritage and culture of the region also impacts the religion, as seen in the contrast between Muslims in the Arab cluster versus Muslims in the Southern Asian cluster. But the driving concern to submit to Allah weaves throughout all the cultural norms in this cluster.

Cultural Value Definitions   Arab

INDIVIDUALISM-COLLECTIVISM   Collectivist
Individualism: Individual goals and rights are more
important than personal relationships.

Collectivism: Personal relationships and benefiting the
group are more important than individual goals.

POWER DISTANCE   High
Low Power Distance: Status differences are of little   Power
importance; empowered decision-making is expected   Distance
across all levels.

High Power Distance: Status differences should shape
social interactions; those with authority should make
decisions.

UNCERTAINTY AVOIDANCE	Moderate

UNCERTAINTY AVOIDANCE

Low Uncertainty Avoidance: Focus on flexibility and adaptability; tolerant of unstructured and unpredictable situations.

High Uncertainty Avoidance: Focus on planning and reliability; uncomfortable with unstructured or unpredictable situations.

Moderate Uncertainty Avoidance

COOPERATIVE-COMPETITITVE

Cooperative: Emphasis on cooperation and nurturing behavior; high value placed on relationships and family.

Competitive: Emphasis on assertive behavior and competition; high value placed on work, task accomplishment, and achievement.

Moderate Cooperative

TIME ORIENTATION

Short-Term: Values Immediate outcomes more than long-term benefits (success now).

Long-Term: Values long-term planning; willing to sacrifice short-term outcomes for long-term benefits (success later).

Short-Term Time

CONTEXT

Low Context: Values direct communication; emphasis on explicit words.

High Context: Values indirect communication; emphasis on harmonic relationships and implicit understanding.

High Context

BEING-DOING

Being: Social commitments and task completion are equally important; diffuse boundaries between personal and work activities.

Doing: Task completion takes precedence over social commitments; clear separation of personal and work activities.

Being

See Appendix B for comparison with other clusters.

All of the cultural value dimensions have relevance for understanding the Arab cluster, but the following are particularly significant for interacting with cultural intelligence when encountering people from the countries in this cluster.

Collectivism

People living across the Arab cluster are Collectivist and as with most Collectivist cultures, the family is the most important basis of group identity, the key social unit. This family loyalty influences all other aspects of an Arab's life. Most Arabs also value friendship and spending time with social acquaintances, but honoring, respecting, and devoting time to one's family and kin is most important.

The family model is very patriarchal and hierarchal (High Power Distance). The fathers and elder men dominate the family—and for a typical Arab, the larger the family, the better. Large families are believed to provide economic benefits, particularly given the probability that children will care for their parents in their elder years. In fact, in some of these countries, if your children don't take care of you, you can take them to court! Large families also provide the father with the prestige of virility. Business visitors will often be invited to a family meal, albeit usually only the men in the family, because there's a high value placed on seeing how the visitor interacts and is accepted within the family unit.

After loyalty to one's family comes loyalty to one's clan; only after that comes one's national identity. There's a limited degree of nationalism and patriotism among many Arabs; instead, there's far greater pride in one's family, clan, and religion.

Short-Term Time Orientation

The Arab cluster has a Short-Term Time Orientation, where the focus is on the present and the immediate future much more than around the long-term future. With an "Inshallah" mindset—where you submissively accept whatever God has sovereignly orchestrated—there's little need to develop long-range plans.

Islam also teaches about the importance of initiative and personal responsibility, but this always seems to be somewhat subordinate to an acceptance that the future has already been determined, so there's little one can do to change it. There's a sense of fate that comes with viewing the future.

Being

The Arab cluster is highly oriented toward the Being side of the Being-Doing continuum. Life is approached somewhat passively, always ensuring that there is time for one's family and enjoying life. This doesn't mean an absence of activity and achievement across the cultures. In fact, there's a long historical precedent of Arab merchants traveling and selling goods around the world. You'll meet industrious Arab business people and shopkeepers in nearly every place you visit globally. But within this cluster, there's a heightened orientation toward social commitments and personal relationships rather than simply being focused upon task completion and accomplishments.

Key Differences

The diversity across the Arab cluster begins with the terrain. The cluster includes vast swaths of dessert, but it also includes the Mediterranean shores of Morocco and the stunning mountains in Oman.

The dress varies widely among Arab people as well. The headdress pattern of a man's outfit is often an indicator of which tribe, clan, or country he comes from. Women are required to wear an abaya—a loose black robe—and head covering in Saudi Arabia, whereas the women in Jordan or Egypt are more likely to dress like women in most other places around the globe. Men are forbidden from drinking alcohol entirely in Saudi Arabia, but in Oman, a man is permitted to order alcohol in a restaurant as long as his head is covered.

The Middle East includes very conservative places like Saudi Arabia and Yemen alongside progressive places like the United Arab Emirates. And somewhere in between are countries like Oman that have strived to retain some of their historical identity while also putting out the welcome mat to foreign visitors and investment.

 Do's and Taboos

- Be respectful during the daily prayer times. Do not stand or walk in front of someone who is praying.

- Avoid eating, drinking, or smoking during the day for the month of Ramadan. If you want to do any of these things, do them in the privacy of your room.

- Do not have the bottom of your shoe facing someone. For example, be careful that, when your legs are crossed, the sole of your shoe does not face upwards toward the person you are conversing with.

- Respect the cultural norms regarding men and women—you don't have to agree with them, but be respectful. Women will often socialize in rooms separate from men. Avoid extended eye contact or shaking hands with the opposite sex unless they initiate it.

- Keep in mind that most Muslims won't eat pork or drink alcohol. And they'll only eat food prepared in accordance with the teachings of the Koran—halal food.

- Avoid using your left hand.

- Remember that not every Arab is Muslim nor will they all fit these descriptions! As always, use these generalizations as a starting point and watch for exceptions.

CONCLUSION

It's been a whirlwind tour through the ten major cultural clusters around the globe. And this is the way we often experience them: A two-day meeting in London, lunch with someone from Dubai, and watching a 90-second news segment about China. There's no substitute for getting to know specific cultures up close—and better yet, getting to know people for who they are as individuals. But life in our fast-paced, globalized world requires that we move in and out of many different cultural contexts all day long. So having a grasp of these general, overarching clusters is a starting point for improving our effectiveness at working and relating across borders.

Understanding the cultural customs and values of these ten cultural clusters doesn't ensure that you'll be able to effectively interact and adapt to the people in these cultures. Cultural intelligence requires more than just knowledge. But having a grasp of the overall patterns and trends that exist across these major cultural clusters is one of the best ways to improve your CQ Knowledge.

To make the most of this understanding, let me leave you with a few guidelines as you continue your own travel in and out of these clusters:

1. Use Cultural Knowledge to Make Predictions
This cursory knowledge about the general background, values, and customs of these clusters can help you predict how people in the different clusters are likely to speak, act, negotiate, and make decisions—but be prepared for your predictions to be wrong. There's diversity within every culture and you'll meet individuals who don't fit the norms. Keep your predictions to yourself. And be ready to adjust your understanding in light of your real-life observations and interactions.

2. Interact with Individuals, Not Cultures
Culture is just a filter people use to perceive and interpret the world around them, and guide their interactions and behavior. It's a powerful filter and usually subconscious. But, as I stated at the outset, few individuals are exact representations of their cultures. There are Southern Asians who are Low Power Distance and Anglos who are Collectivist. Move as quickly as possible beyond broad cultural stereotypes to get to know individuals in their own right. The same applies when you're getting to know a specific organization. Use this information as a starting point, then expand and adjust your knowledge as you go along.

3. Improve Your Overall CQ
Cultural intelligence includes your motivation (CQ Drive), understanding (CQ Knowledge), planning (CQ Strategy), and behavioral adaptability (CQ Action). Learning about these ten cultural clusters is primarily related to

improving your CQ Knowledge, but it can certainly help you plan and be more aware in the midst of intercultural encounters (CQ Strategy) as well. This cultural understanding has limited value, however, if it isn't integrated with all four capabilities of cultural intelligence. For example, knowing that harmony is an important value in Confucian Asia is essential, but your cultural intelligence is demonstrated by whether you can effectively negotiate a deal that is both respectful and effective with someone from China. (See Appendix A for more on cultural intelligence).

4. Assess Your CQ and Personal Value Preferences

If you haven't already done so, take the CQ Assessment to learn more about your CQ strengths and to see where you need work to improve your CQ. The assessment results will also reveal your personal preferences along the seven cultural-value orientations we've examined throughout this book. Then you can compare your personal preferences with the predominant value orientations of each of these ten clusters. Visit www.culturalQ.com for more information on the assessments available.

I hope this global journey across the ten cultural clusters has further piqued your interest in understanding the vastly different ways people around the world think and behave. The tendency of some people is to de-emphasize differences and focus upon what we all have in common. There are certainly commonalities among all of us as human beings, and it's Important to recognize that. But some of the most helpful insights, opportunities for growth, and potential lie in our differences; diverse perspectives plus cultural intelligence leads to better solutions for all of us.

Thanks for joining me on this journey toward a more culturally intelligent world.

Further Reading and/or Listening

Ten Clusters

Customs of the World: Using Cultural Intelligence to Adapt Wherever You Are (Great Courses Audio/Video Course) by David Livermore

- This 24-lecture course devotes one 30-minute lecture to each of the ten cultural clusters. In addition, the course looks at ten cultural value dimensions and explores how this information relates to developing your overall cultural intelligence. (www.thegreatcourses.com)

Culture, Leadership, and Organizations (Sage) by House, Hanges, Javidan, Dorfman, & Gupta

- This book reports on the GLOBE leadership study, the most comprehensive study to date on leadership similarities and differences across the world. The book specifically looks at the leadership practices across the ten cultural clusters.

Cultural Intelligence

The Cultural Intelligence Difference (AMACOM) by David Livermore

- This book is packed with dozens of strategies for improving all four CQ capabilities. It's primarily oriented toward helping individuals improve their CQ.

Handbook of Cultural Intelligence (M.E. Sharpe) edited by Soon Ang and Linn Van Dyne

- This book is the most comprehensive collection of research on cultural intelligence from various scholars around the world.

Leading with Cultural Intelligence (AMACOM) by David Livermore

- This book is a practical explanation of the cultural intelligence model and specifically applies it to leadership.

Acknowledgments

Most of my books begin as conversations with friends, colleagues, and people I meet while traveling around the world. This one is no exception. In recent years, people have been asking me, "Where should we begin to learn more about different cultures?" Others challenged me when I downplayed the value of lists of "Do's and Taboos." And others pushed me to think about what cultural knowledge might be most helpful for giving individuals the big picture. This is my small contribution to those conversations.

I'd like to extend enormous thanks to the colleagues across the globe who read early drafts of this and offered their expertise on one or more of the clusters. I'm sure some readers will still balk at some of the descriptions of various cultures, and I welcome that kind of interaction. This is not an exact science. But there would have been far more uproar without the thoughtful contributions of: Soon Ang, Steve Argue, Anindita Banerjee, Vanessa Barros Jones, Ismael Koshy, Marina Lazaro, Anastasia Nekrasova, Kok Yee Ng, Dennis Nørmark, Nadja Paffenholz, Neil Prentice, Devina Raditya, Amy Richey, Cecilia Ronderos, Regula Sindemann, Mark Tittley, and Daniel Wong.

Thank you also to our growing team at the Cultural Intelligence Center. I get far too much of the credit for the work we all do together. And, in particular, thank you to my colleague and business partner, Linn Van Dyne, who owned this with me from the beginning and, as always, pushes me to do one more edit to make it better. And thanks to Julie Slagter, who played a crucial role in managing this project to completion and who, more importantly, shares a commitment with me to cultural intelligence.

Emily and Grace. I used to thrive on teaching you about the world. Now you push me to think differently about the world you've inherited.

Linda. Has it really been 20 years? Time flies when you're married to your best friend.

Appendix A: What's Your CQ?

Why is it that some people seem extremely comfortable interacting with others who come from different cultures, while others seem like a fish out of water? Is it merely a matter of who has experience and who doesn't, or is there something more to it? This is the area that has piqued my interest for the last several years, and it is the foundation of our research on cultural intelligence, or CQ, the capability to be effective in any culture.

The world includes gifted musicians, athletes, economists, and writers. In the same way, some people are culturally intelligent—that is, they have the gift of effectively interacting and working with people from diverse cultures. But cultural intelligence isn't a natural born trait. It's a set of capabilities that most anyone can develop and learn.

Who Are the Culturally Intelligent?

Individuals with high CQ can effectively adapt to various multicultural situations. And they possess strength in four distinct CQ capabilities—CQ Drive, CQ Knowledge, CQ Strategy, and CQ Action. All four capabilities are needed, because focusing on one without the others may actually result in increased cultural ignorance rather than enhanced cultural intelligence. This is because CQ requires an overall repertoire of adaptive capabilities.

Here's a brief description of these four CQ capabilities and some examples of how they relate to working and relating cross-culturally.

CQ Drive

CQ Drive refers to whether or not you have the confidence and drive to work through the challenges and conflict that often accompany intercultural work. The ability to be personally engaged and to persevere through intercultural challenges is one of the most novel aspects of cultural intelligence. Many intercultural training approaches simply assume that people are motivated to gain cross-cultural capabilities. Yet employees often approach diversity training apathetically, and employees headed out on international assignments are often more concerned about moving their families overseas and getting settled than they are about developing cultural understanding. Without ample motivation, there's little point in spending time and money on training.

Doug, an American with a multinational firm who was sent to manage a team in Bangkok, describes how little attention he paid to the cultural training he received before moving to Thailand. It wasn't that he didn't care. It's just that he was overwhelmed getting ready for the move and he found the training overly theoretical and too focused upon cultural stereotypes. But he definitely wanted to succeed.

CQ Drive includes: intrinsic motivation—the degree to which you derive enjoyment from culturally diverse situations; extrinsic motivation—

the tangible benefits you gain from culturally diverse experiences; and, self-efficacy—your confidence that you will be effective in an intercultural encounter. All three of these motivational dynamics play a role in how you approach multicultural situations. Stop and examine your motivation for doing cross-cultural work. Your CQ Drive is strongly related to your effectiveness in new cultural contexts.

CQ Knowledge

CQ Knowledge is the cognitive dimension of cultural intelligence. It refers to your level of understanding about culture and culture's role in shaping the way to interact when different cultures are involved. Your CQ Knowledge is based upon the degree to which you understand the idea of culture and how it influences the way you think and behave. It also includes your overall understanding of the ways cultures vary from one context to the next.

When Doug got to Bangkok, he quickly discovered that leading and motivating his mostly Asian team wasn't coming easily. Although he had a reputation for being a phenomenal negotiator, his negotiations kept getting stalled. Even though he had extensive management experience, he was losing confidence in his ability to be a good leader here.

One of the most important parts of CQ Knowledge is a macro understanding of cultural systems, and the cultural norms and values associated with different societies. In order to lead effectively you need to understand ways that communication styles, predomInant religious beliefs, role expectations for men and women, etc., can differ across cultures. In addition, general knowledge about different types of economic, business, legal, and political systems that exist throughout the world is important. And you need a core understanding of culture, language patterns, and non-verbal behaviors. This kind of knowledge helps build your confidence when working in a new cultural environment.

The other important part of CQ Knowledge is knowing how culture influences your effectiveness in specific domains. For example, being an effective global leader in business looks different from being an effective leader of a multicultural university. And working across borders for an information technology company requires a different application of cultural understanding than working across borders for a charitable organization or on a military initiative. This kind of specialized, domain-specific cultural knowledge, combined with a macro understanding of cultural issues, is a crucial part of leading with cultural intelligence.

CQ Knowledge is the area that is most often emphasized in typical approaches to intercultural competency. A large and growing training and consulting industry focuses on teaching people about cultural values. While valuable, however, the understanding that comes from CQ Knowledge has to be combined with the other three capabilities of CQ or its relevance to the real demands of leadership is questionable and potentially detrimental.

CQ Strategy

CQ Strategy refers to your level of awareness and ability to strategize when crossing cultures. This capability involves slowing down the rpm's long enough to carefully observe what's going on inside your own and other people's heads. It's the ability to think about your own thought processes, and draw upon your cultural knowledge to understand a different cultural context and solve problems in that situation. It includes whether we can use our cultural knowledge to plan an appropriate strategy, accurately interpret what's going on in an intercultural situation, and check to see if our expectations are accurate or need to be adjusted.

Doug has always used a leadership style focused on developing individuals to pursue their personal goals and to "lead themselves." He was aware that this was a countercultural approach in Asia, but he had no interest in becoming a highly directive leader. So he had to develop a strategy for how to be true to himself while effectively leading a team with values different from his.

Seasoned leaders often jump into meetings and new situations with little planning. This often works fine when meeting with colleagues or clients from a similar cultural background. By drawing on emotional intelligence and leadership experience, we can often get away with "winging it" because we know how to respond to cues and how to talk about projects. When meetings involve individuals from different cultural contexts, however, many of the rules change. Relying upon our ability to intuitively respond to cues in these more novel situations is dangerous. That's where CQ Strategy comes in.

CQ Strategy includes planning, awareness, and checking. Planning is taking the time to prepare for an intercultural encounter—anticipating how to approach the people, topic, and situation. Awareness means being in tune with what's going on in one's self and others during the interaction. And checking is the monitoring we do as we engage in interactions to see if the plans and expectations we had were appropriate. It's comparing what we expected with our actual experience. CQ Strategy emphasizes implementation, and it's the lynchpin that connects understanding cultural issues to actually being able to use that understanding to manage effectively.

CQ Action

Finally, CQ Action is your ability to act appropriately in a wide range of cultural situations. It influences whether we can actually accomplish our performance goals effectively in light of different cultural situations. One of the most important aspects of CQ Action is knowing when to adapt to another culture and when not to do so. A leader with high CQ learns which actions will and won't enhance effectiveness, and acts upon that understanding. Thus, CQ Action involves flexible behaviors tailored to the specific cultural context.

Doug is grateful for staff who are fluent in English; he's learning some basic Thai to get along. But at times, he feels like he has to relearn English, too. His assistant needs very explicit, step-by-step directions. And on the rare occasion when she makes a request, he has the hardest time figuring out exactly what she's asking for.

CQ Action includes the capability to be flexible in verbal and nonverbal actions. It also includes appropriate flexibility in speech acts—the exact words and phrases we use when we communicate specific types of messages (e.g. offering negative feedback directly or indirectly, or knowing how to appropriately make a request).

While the demands of today's intercultural settings make it impossible to master all the do's and don'ts of various cultures, there are certain behaviors that should be modified when we interact with different cultures. For example, Westerners need to learn the importance of carefully studying business cards presented by those from most Asian contexts. Also, some basic verbal and nonverbal behaviors enhance the extent to which others see us as effective. As an example, the verbal tone (e.g., loud vs. soft) in which words are spoken can convey different meanings across cultures. And although it is not necessary for an outsider to master the intricacies of bowing in Japan, appropriate use of touch is something to bear in mind. In sum, almost every approach to intercultural work has insisted on the importance of flexibility. With CQ Action, we now have a way to enhance flexibility.

Improving Your CQ

Your CQ can improve. It's something anyone can develop and learn, assuming they have the interest in doing so. A few basic ways to get started include the following:

Reflect on your CQ: Begin with a commitment to consider your capabilities for working and relating across cultures. By thinking through the four capabilities of CQ, consider which areas are strongest and weakest for you.

CQ Drive: What's my level of interest in cross-cultural issues?

CQ Knowledge: To what degree do I understand how cultures are similar and different?

CQ Strategy: Am I aware of what's occurring in a cross-cultural situation and am I able to plan accordingly?

CQ Action: Do I know when I should adapt and when I should not adapt my behavior cross-culturally?

Each of us is stronger in some of these areas than others. Zero in on one specific CQ capability to begin increasing your overall CQ.

Assess Your CQ: There are a variety of academically validated CQ assessments that are proven to predict the degree to which you are able to function effectively in intercultural contexts. The CQ Self-Assessment is a great way to begin developing awareness by reflecting on your intercultural abilities. As a next step, the CQ Multi-Rater Assessment can be used as a 360-degree instrument that allows bosses, peers, direct reports, clients, and sometimes even family members to assess you according to the four CQ capabilities and the sub-dimensions of each. Find more information about these and other CQ assessments at www.culturalQ.com.

Hands-On Experiences: There's no substitute for "on-the-job training" when it comes to improving your CQ. The ideal scenario is when you have a chance to travel internationally and get immersed in a local culture. Whether you're traveling for work, pleasure, or as a charitable volunteer, be sure to wander from the touristy spots. Even if you're staying at the Shangri-La in downtown Bangkok, you can jump on a bus and suddenly be immersed in true local culture. This gives you a whole different insight into Thai culture than what you'll get from the hotel lobby or Starbucks.

There's an abundance of opportunities for hands-on experiences closer to home too. Chances are, there are growing numbers of people from different cultures living nearby. For example, the U.S. census data just reported that the U.S. now has 50 million Hispanics—more than the entire population of Spain. Although many Hispanic-Americans live in coastal cities or closer to the border, even my little Midwest city in Michigan has grown from three percent Hispanic 15 years ago to 17 percent Hispanic today! If you're in a community where there's still relatively little ethnic diversity, seek out interactions with people who come from a different subculture religiously, politically, or generationally.

Or, gain some hands-on-experience by pulling together a cross-functional team with people from marketing, engineering, and IT. Working together with people from these kinds of diverse "subcultures" can also play a role in increasing your CQ. Individuals who are part of culturally diverse groups are more likely to havehigh CQ than those who remain isolated with individuals like themselves. It sounds obvious, but it's amazing how often work groups and social gatherings miss out on the rich resource available to them through hands-on experiences with diverse colleagues and friends.

Personal Development Plan: Once you have a good idea of where your greatest CQ strengths and weaknesses lie, you can put together a development plan for improving your CQ. The research on CQ has revealed several proven strategies for how to use your CQ strengths and how to enhance other CQ capabilities (Drive, Knowledge, Strategy, and Action). Many of these strategies may not strike you as rocket-science (e.g., name your biases, study a new language, manage your expectations, etc.) but they're proven to increase your effectiveness in culturally diverse situations. We often overlook some of the obvious ways to tap into things we already do to also improve the ways we interact and work cross-culturally.

Identify something you can do in the next week to help you improve in one of the four CQ capabilities (Drive, Knowledge, Strategy, Action). How about the next month? Six months? Year? Write down your plan, share it with someone, and have them offer you feedback.

Take a Class: Learning about culture through books and classes is NOT a sure way to improve CQ. In fact, someone who only learns about culture academically may actually have lower CQ than someone who hasn't taken any formal courses on culture and diversity. Cerebral understanding about culture without the corresponding motivation and strategy can actually be detrimental to your overall CQ. You might think you are culturally intelligent and actually have little common sense for how to apply the cultural knowledge you've learned academically.

When combined with the other CQ capabilities, studying about culture and global events through a class—either a formal university course or a workshop offered by your organization—can improve your CQ. This benefit can be tapped even from a class that doesn't directly relate to culture and diversity. Simply exercising the brain to think critically and strategically can play a role in how you improve your overall CQ. When you devote focused attention to studying the role of culture in the world and interact with others about it, it's another powerful way to enhance your cultural intelligence.

A Better Way
Despite millions of dollars spent on cultural sensitivity training and diversity programs, little has improved in the way many individuals and companies are actually behaving when it comes to working across borders—whether with the person in the cubicle next door or a client 12 time zones away.

Respect and sensitivity are non-negotiable values, but we have to go beyond those ideals to actually find ways to successfully adapt to various cultural situations while still remaining true to ourselves. The cultural intelligence research and model is uniquely suited to address this need.

Begin by finding out what your CQ is, or, more importantly, which CQ capabilities are strongest and weakest for you. Then gain the benefits that comes from improving your CQ while simultaneously treating people with respect and dignity—and in turn, make the world a better place for all of us.

Appendix B: Cultural Value Dimensions and Clusters

Cultural Value Dimensions

Individualism: Individual goals and rights are more important than personal relationship.
Collectivism: Personal relationships and benefiting the group are more important than individual goals.

Low Power Distance: Status differences are of little importance; empowered decision-making is expected across all levels.
High Power Distance: Status differences should shape social interactions; those with authority should make decisions.

Low Uncertainty Avoidance: Focus on flexibility and adaptability; tolerant of unstructured and unpredictable situations.
High Uncertainty Avoidance: Focus on planning and reliability; uncomfortable with unstructured or unpredictable situations.

Cooperative: Emphasis upon cooperation and nurturing behavior; high value placed upon relationships and family.
Competitive: Emphasis upon assertive behavior and competition; high value placed upon work, task accomplishment, and achievement.

Short Term: Values immediate outcomes more than long-term benefits (success now).
Long Term: Values long term planning; willing to sacrifice short-term outcomes for long-term benefits (success later).

Low Context: Values direct communication. Emphasis on explicit words.
High Context: Values indirect communication. Emphasis on implicit understanding.

Being: Social Commitments and task completion are equally important; diffuse boundaries between personal and work activities.
Doing: Task completion takes precedence over social commitments; clear separation of personal and work activities.

Cultural Clusters

Nordic Europe: Denmark, Finland, Norway, Sweden, etc.
Anglo: Australia, Canada, New Zealand, U.K., U.S., etc.
Germanic Europe: Austria, Belgium, Germany, Netherlands, German Switzerland, etc.
Eastern Europe: Bulgaria, Czech Republic, Estonia, Hungary, Kazakhstan, Poland, Russia, Serbia, etc.
Latin Europe: France, French Canada, Latin Switzerland, Italy, Portugal, Spain, etc.
Latin America: Argentina, Brazil, Chile, Colombia, Costa Rica, Ecuador, Mexico, Venezuela, etc.
Confucian Asia: China, Hong Kong, Japan, Singapore, South Korea, Taiwan, etc.
Southern Asia: India, Indonesia, Malaysia, Philippines, Thailand, etc.
Sub-Saharan Africa: Ghana, Kenya, Namibia, Nigeria, Zambia, Zimbabwe, etc.
Arab: Bahrain, Egypt, Kuwait, Libya, Morocco, Qatar, Saudi Arabia, Tunisia, U.A.E., etc.

INDIVIDUALISM — COLLECTIVISM

Anglo Germanic Nordic	Eastern Europe Latin Europe	Arab Southern Asia* Confucian Asia Latin America Sub-Saharan Africa

LOW POWER DISTANCE — HIGH POWER DISTANCE

Anglo Germanic Nordic	Confucian Asia Eastern Europe* Latin Europe Sub-Saharan Africa	Arab Latin America Southern Asia*

LOW UNCERTAINTY AVOIDANCE — HIGH UNCERTAINTY AVOIDANCE

Anglo Eastern Europe Nordic	Arab Confucian Asia* Germanic Southern Asia* Sub-Saharan Africa	Latin Europe Latin America

COOPERATIVE — COMPETITIVE

Nordic Sub-Saharan Africa	Arab Southern Asia* Confucian Asia Eastern Europe Latin America Latin Europe	Anglo Germanic

SHORT TERM — LONG TERM

Anglo Arab Eastern Europe Nordic Sub-Saharan Africa	Germanic Latin America Latin Europe Southern Asia*	Confucian Asia

LOW CONTEXT — HIGH CONTEXT

Anglo Germanic Nordic	Eastern Europe Latin America Latin Europe	Arab Confucian Asia Southern Asia* Sub-Saharan Africa

BEING ORIENTATION — DOING ORIENTATION

Arab Latin America Nordic Sub-Saharan Africa	Confucian Asia* Eastern Europe Latin Europe Southern Asia*	Anglo Germanic

*Significant variation within cluster

Notes

Introduction

1. Ang, Soon, & Van Dyne, Linn (2008). *Handbook of Cultural Intelligence: Theory, Measurement, and Applications.* Armonk, NY: M.E. Sharpe, 2008, 3.
2. Ronen, Simcha & Shenkar, Oded. (1985). Clustering Countries on Attitudinal Dimensions: A Review and Synthesis. *Academy of Management Review, 10,* 435-447.
3. House, R.J., Hanges, P. J., Javidan, M., Dorman, P. W. & Gupta, V. (2004). *Culture, Leadership, and Organizations: The GLOBE Study of 62 Societies.* Thousand Oaks, CA: Sage, 2004.
4. Osland, Joyce, & Bird, Allan. (2000). Beyond Sophisticated Stereotyping: Cultural Sensemaking in Context. *Academy of Management Executive 14,* 1:65-80.

Chapter 1. Nordic

1. Bling is a contemporary term used to refer to flamboyant or ostentatious clothing or jewelry
2. Be sure to check out *Cultural Intelligence for Stone Age Brains by Dennis Normark* (Copenhagen: Gyldendal Business, 2013).

Chapter 2. Anglo

1. Ashkanasy, Neal M, Trevor-Roberts, Edwin, & Earnshaw, Louise. (2002). The Anglo Cluster: Legacy of the British Empire. *Journal of World Business, 37,* 1, 28–39.
2. Darwin, John. (2012). *Unfinished Empire: The Global Expansion of Britain.* London: Allen Dale Publ.
3. Baxter Black. (2011) Veteran's Day. *Tri-State Livestock News,* http://www.tsln.com/article/20111208/TSLN04/111209977, accessed November 2, 2012.

Chapter 3. Germanic

1. Szabo, Erna, Brodbeck, Felix C. Den Hartog, Deanne N. ,Reber, Gerhard, Weibler, Jürgen & Wunderer, Rolf. (2002). The Germanic Europe Cluster: Where Employees Have a Voice. *Journal of World Business 37,* 1, 55-68.
2. Ibid.

Chapter 4. Eastern Europe

1. Bakacsi, Gyula, Sándor, Takács, Andras, Karácsonyi, & Viktor, Imrek. (2002). Eastern European Cluster: Tradition and Transition. *Journal of World Business* 37, 1, 69-80.

Chapter 5. Latin Europe

1. Beardsley, Eleanor. (2012). Outsourced croissants enrage traditional French bakers. National Public radio, http://www.npr.org/blogs/thesalt/2012/08/07/158371114/outsourced-croissants-outrage-traditional-french-bakers, accessed August 12, 2012.
2. Weber, Max. (2012). *The Theory of Social and Economic Organization*. Eastford, CT: Martino Fine Books, 130-131.
3. Jesuino, Jorge Correia. (2002). Latin Europe Cluster: From South to North. *Journal of World Business* 37, 1, 81-89.

Chapter 6. Latin America

1. Pew Forum. (2013). Conclave elects Pope Francis, http://www.pewforum.org/Christian/ Catholic/Conclave-elects-Pope-Francis.aspx, accessed March 14, 2013.

Chapter 7. Confucian Asia

1. Prothero, Stephen. (2010). *God is Not One: The Eight Rival Religions that Run the World and Why Their Differences Matter*. San Francisco: Harper One.
2. Lee Kuan Yew. (2000). *From Third World to First: The Singapore Story: 1965-2000* New York: Harper Books, 175.

Chapter 10. Arab

1. Prothero, Stephen. (2010). *God is Not One: The Eight Rival Religions that Run the World and Why Their Differences Matter*. San Francisco: Harper One.

Made in the USA
San Bernardino, CA
22 December 2018